"Price may be the best living religious writer and is one of the best reasons I know of to consider becoming a Christian."

—*The Boston Globe*

"Brilliant and moving apocryphal gospel stories."

—*Publishers Weekly*, starred review

"It is good to have an outlaw storyteller like Reynolds Price turn up from time to time to help us reimagine gospel truth."

—*The Christian Century*

"Provocative and insightful."

—*The Dallas Morning News*

"An insightful work combining thoughtful erudition with Price's obvious love for the Gospel stories and his expansive artistic abilities, resulting in a text designed to help readers see anew Jesus of Nazareth."

—*Los Angeles Times*

"The results of his work are certain to provoke debate. They are also . . . lucid, intelligent, never self-serving."

—*Booklist*

A SERIOUS WAY
OF WONDERING

BOOKS BY

REYNOLDS PRICE

REYNOLDS PRICE

A SERIOUS WAY OF WONDERING

THE ETHICS OF JESUS IMAGINED

SCRIBNER

NEW YORK   LONDON   TORONTO   SYDNEY

SCRIBNER
1230 Avenue of the Americas
New York, NY 10020

First Scribner trade paperback edition 2006

SCRIBNER and design are trademarks
of Macmillan Library Reference USA, Inc., used under license
by Simon & Schuster, the publisher of this work.

For information about special discounts for bulk purchases,
please contact Simon & Schuster Special Sales: 1-800-456-6798 or
business@simonandschuster.com

Text set in Electra

Manufactured in the United States of America

1   3   5   7   9   10   8   6   4   2

Library of Congress Cataloging-in-Publication Data
Price, Reynolds, 1933–
A serious way of wondering : the ethics of Jesus imagined /
Reynolds Price.
p.   cm.
Includes bibliographical references.
1. Jesus Christ—Ethics. 2. Christian ethics. I. Title.
BS2417.E8P75 2003
241—dc21   2003041506

ISBN-13: 978-0-7432-3008-7
ISBN-10: 0-7432-3008-6
ISBN-13: 978-0-7432-3009-4 (Pbk)
ISBN-10: 0-7432-3009-4 (Pbk)

A portion of this work, appearing on pages 92–94,
was previously published in Time as "Jesus of Nazareth—
An Untold Story," copyright © 1999 by Time, Inc.
Reprinted by permission.

CONTENTS

A SERIOUS WAY
OF WONDERING

PREFACE

T hough I'm not a churchgoer, for more than sixty years I've read widely in the life and teachings of Jesus; and since at least the age of nine, I've thought of myself as a Christian. This book comes ultimately from those beginnings, but it has a more immediate cause. An explanation will permit me a brief good memory.

As I approach my seventieth birthday, I revert with a special frequency to scenes from early summers (fall and winter have often been grim). One of the best of those stretches was a time I spent at Harvard University when I was twenty-one. In 1954, for two months between my junior and senior years at Duke, I lived through both summer terms on the first floor of Stoughton Hall in the Yard; and I took swift and bracingly rigorous courses in modern American fiction and Victorian poetry (I also audited courses in French Impressionism and European Nationalism). Cambridge, like the other port cities of east-coast America, is a humid swamp from June into late September; but as a North Carolina native, born long before air-conditioning crazed my genetic thermostat, I was impervious and relished attending each morning's lectures, then returning to a well-baked dormitory room, stripping to my shorts, crashing on a sodden bed and reading for unbroken blissful hours—more bookish-hours-per-day than I've navigated before or since. Though I'd consumed books from the first grade onward, at the age of full adulthood I was suddenly like a starved man whose only available food was words and who was steadily happy to consume them as vital, if intoxicating, fuel. My will to be a writer, which I'd shakily announced from the age of sixteen, fined its point to a durable hardness then and there (the fact that I noted Horatio Alger as a former occupant of Stoughton Hall was a cheerful help).

So I felt a pleasing arc begin to form when, forty-six years later, the Reverend Peter Gomes asked me to deliver the next annual Francis Greenwood Peabody Lecture at Harvard's Memorial Church. I was soon interested to learn that Peabody (1847–1936) had served as a Unitarian minister before returning to Harvard, his alma mater, where he distinguished himself for intro-ducing the study of social ethics and ultimately a Department of Social Ethics (his course was known to students as "Peabo's drainage, drunkenness, and divorce"). It seemed appropriate therefore to give the next Peabody Lecture, to what I assumed would be a largely undergraduate audience, on a subject that had long concerned me—the ethics of Jesus of Nazareth.

I was planning to teach, soon again, a seminar which I've taught for a number of years at Duke

University—a study of the Gospels of Mark and John—and since the final paper in that course requires each student to write an apocryphal gospel and since I'd only recently written, at the suggestion of *Time* magazine, a group of apocryphal scenes from the life of Jesus,* I decided to conclude my lecture with a further narrative exploration of a moment in which Jesus is confronted by an enduringly significant ethical dilemma which the four Gospels never bring before him. I'd after all spent a great part of my life as a writer of fictional and autobiographical narratives; and I knew that the act of telling a story, especially a story invented as one tells it, can sometimes become a moral discovery or (as any child knows) a private vision that approaches revelation in intensity and personal usefulness.

In Cambridge then in April 2001, I was received generously by the Reverend Gomes, his Associate Minister the Reverend Dorothy Austin and the staff of the Memorial Church; and I spoke in that resonant sanctuary on a Saturday morning before an audience which

---

Apocryphal, in this case, has no connotations of *false* or *untrue*. As with the other gospels referred to below as *apocryphal*, it means *not canonical*, not accepted by the orthodox churches as sufficiently reliable for inclusion in services of worship or in private devotion—therefore *hidden away*, the literal Greek sense of the word. I've gone so far as to publish an apocryphal gospel of my own, in my *Three Gospels* (Scribner); and each student in my annual Duke University seminar on the Gospels of Mark and John writes his or her own apocryphal gospel—an attempt to describe what seems essential from the life and work of Jesus of Nazareth in no more than 11,300 words (the length of the Gospel of Mark).

included both a gratifying number of students—considering the day and the hour—and the Church's imposing Board of Visitors. The fictional story with which I concluded is the first of the three stories included here. It not only concerned a dilemma of personal importance to me, its dilemma was—and still is—one which troubles millions and continues to torment the institutions of Christianity today. In my narrative, Jesus is confronted with homosexuality when, risen from the tomb on Easter morning, he searches for and finds Judas Iscariot, the disciple who'd handed him over to his enemies and assured his agonized death. All that remains for the burnt-out Judas to reveal is a passionate love for Jesus, a love which—foiled, he claims—led him to betray the teacher he'd followed so longingly.

Five months after my visit to Cambridge, on 26 September 2001—two weeks after some three thousand human lives were destroyed in the World Trade Center, the Pentagon and on an airplane in Pennsylvania—I kept a commitment to speak at the National Cathedral in Washington. In the heart of that vast cavern, at a time when every famous American building seemed a dangerous place—a living organism of almost hopeless fragility—I began to speak at an evening hour which marked the commencement of Yom Kippur. As I began by noting that loaded coincidence—and remarking how earnestly we as Americans (Jew and Gentile and whoever else) needed not only to acknowledge our grief for the recent tragedy but also for the wrongs committed by our nation against others—I realized that the thousand people who sat before me were hardly present, on a weeknight, to hear me but were responding to a need to gather in sacred space. I went on to give them a further developed version of my sense of Jesus' ethics (including, in the circumstances, a renewed conviction of his pacifism). And I added a second fictional scene in which Jesus encounters another crisis he never meets in the Gospels—suicide, a perpetual urgency in virtually all societies. The traitor Judas is determined to kill himself, and the risen Jesus is beside him in his intention.

Since that night, and the discussion which followed with an understandably intense audience and the Cathedral's kind and challenging staff, I've gone on expanding my study of a subject which I take to be perennially important. For a version which I presented as the Rudin Lecture in November 2002 at a place which has been especially welcoming on several occasions—Auburn Seminary in New York—I added a third fictional encounter in which Jesus meets, alone, a woman who not only presents him with questions which the Gospels don't offer but likewise confronts his sense of himself in an especially daunting way. What, in a world which controls women so strenuously, is an adulterous and rejected wife and mother to do for the remainder of her life?

In the form published here, I've added numerous passages of reflection, and unorthodox theology, for which I wouldn't want any of my prior hosts, or the audiences who engaged me in probing discussion, to be held responsible. Anyone who's read *Three Gospels* and the subsequent *Letter to a Man in the Fire* will know of my long interest in the life and work of Jesus of Nazareth—his legacy to the world and the legacy which he seized so avidly from the history, faith and scriptures of his people. Those readers will also know that I'm not a priest, a clergyman of any sort or a trained theologian. Yet I'd assure any reader that, though I'm of course subject to errors, accidents and failures of intelligence, I've worked to deal gravely here with such grave matters.

Since I could hardly expect many professional scholars of the New Testament to attend those lectures; and since I hoped then—as I hope now—to reach the widest possible number of listeners and readers, I've offered more explanation than scholars would require and perhaps less than some readers may want. For the latter, I've provided occasional footnotes; and I've included a short list of recommended reading. Throughout, I've tried to indicate moments which I suspect of being new or inescapably radical.

Though I've translated the Gospels of Mark and John from the Greek and published them in *Three Gospels* (the third is my own), all quotations from scripture are given here in the Updated New American Standard Version. While I regret that the American Standard follows the eighteenth-century habit of capitalizing nouns and pronouns referring to God and Jesus (a practice foreign to the Hebrew and Greek originals) and while it over-punctuates texts whose originals bear no punctuation whatever, it remains the most nearly literal translation of the whole Bible that's presently both available and easily readable. Literal translation can sometimes present the reader with difficulties of understanding; but it can almost automatically—as in the King James Version—reveal the astonishing eloquence of the Hebrew, Aramaic and Greek originals. I have not reproduced the New American's scrupulous, but visually confusing, practice of italicizing occasional (and often quite unnecessary) words added to clarify a phrase of the Greek.

Finally, a list of the friends and colleagues whose wisdom and scholarship—going back to my childhood—lie behind my interest in these matters would be longer than the text itself. Seven friends have been of special recent help—Stephen Katz, Jonathan Uslaner, Ryan Sample, Jeffrey Anderson, Susan Moldow, and two eminent colleagues at Duke University: D. Moody Smith and David Aers. They deserve no blame for my errors and have saved me from more than one.

R. P.

1. A POSSIBLE LIFE OF JESUS

The claim that Jesus of Nazareth is the most influential man or woman in history is hardly debatable, nor is the fact that he remains a figure of startling vitality throughout the world. *Startling* because the available facts make the reality all but incredible. Though he died in about the year AD 30, today some 32 percent of the world's population—roughly 1,974,000,000 human beings—claim to be followers of Jesus. And a large share of the world's ongoing politics, economics, art and behavior is unimaginable outside the shadow he casts. No other human being before Muhammad, who was born in about AD 570, endures with any significant fraction of the personal force that Jesus continues to exert (the Buddha's teachings continue their power in many lives, but the facts of his life and his person seem of a lesser force for his followers).

Jesus' acts and his teaching have generated—among those who've called themselves followers—deeds of an otherwise unimaginable selflessness and creative genius as well as pulverizing evil. To note only the latest reactions to evils perpetrated throughout the world in Jesus' name, the recent assaults by Muslim fundamentalists upon Americans and American interests are as demanding of Christian answers as they are tragic. Is some irreducible outrage implicit in the very life and words of Jesus that has not been addressed by his followers?

For a start at least, the single saying of Jesus which—in the hands of self-blinded followers—has fueled the most tragic effects has been his final words in the Gospel of Matthew 28.18–20.

> "All authority has been given to Me in heaven and on earth. Go therefore and make disciples of all the nations, baptizing them in the name of the Father and the Son and the Holy Spirit, teaching them to observe all that I commanded you; and lo, I am with you always, even to the end of the age."

The crusades of the Middle Ages, the European conquest of the Americas and the resulting slaughter and enslavement of millions of indigenous peoples and a great deal of similar Western triumphalism and murderous anti-Semitism are only the largest of those effects. And whether Jesus ever spoke such words—or what he might have intended by them—we'll likely never know (I'll state my own conclusion later).

Given the vitality of his ongoing personal power, in any case, it seems inescapable that an attempt at defining the intentions and the ethics of Jesus should begin by setting out the lines of his life as they've been clarified in a research effort as voluminous as any in the annals of scholarship. It's necessary to stress that the following outline offers my own deductions from a long study of that long effort. Though I might not find many scholars who'd accept my entire outline, I believe it's solidly grounded. And I'd add that the central paradox in the study of Jesus' life resides in the fact that, despite intense scholarly controversies in the past two centuries, the essential lines of our present knowledge were defined in the oldest of the four Gospels—that pamphlet of only some 11,300 Greek words which we call the Gospel of Mark, written in a headlong but eloquent version of the street-and-market Greek called Koine and probably completed almost surely before AD 70, within a short lifetime of Jesus' death.

The Gospel of Matthew says, and the Gospel of Luke implies, that Jesus was born in the reign of King Herod the Great; and Herod died in 4 BC. Before the long-awaited death of that wily monster then, Jesus (or Yeshua bar Miriam as he may have been called in his hometown and in his native Aramaic) was born.* (At the time of his birth, his parents were likely residing some four miles south of Jerusalem in the village of Bethlehem—the hometown of King David, who had

---

*The puzzlement which may arise from discovering that Jesus was born at least four years "BC—before Christ" results from a calendrical miscalculation made by a sixth-century monk named Dionysius Exiguus ("Little Denis"). In Rome, deducing a chronology which is employed even now, he dated the birth of Christ incorrectly; and we are the heirs of his error.

reigned a thousand years earlier. While many students assume that the Gospels assign Jesus' birth to Bethlehem because a prophecy in Micah 5.2 seems to require that Messiah be born there, in fact only Matthew and Luke specify Bethlehem. Mark makes no mention of the birth, and John 7.42 contains a reference to Bethlehem which may indicate John's knowledge of Jesus' birth in David's native city (John has an appetite for irony which makes the reference ambiguous; but I see it as an indication that John knows of, and confirms, the tradition of Jesus' birth in Bethlehem).

Jesus' mother was named Miriam, *Mary* in English; her husband was Yosef or *Joseph*, and they were the heads of an observant Jewish family that included several brothers and sisters. Apart from the tradition in Matthew and Luke that Jesus was born of a virgin mother, there are other traces of evidence that there was something peculiar about his origins. When he returns to his family's home in the midst of his wandering career—since his birth, they've moved north to Galilee—the locals refer to him in Mark 6.3 as "the son of Mary," which is odd enough (why not the customary "son of Joseph," even if Joseph is dead by then?).

Does the phrase suggest perhaps that, in his village, Jesus was even considered a bastard child—or at least one whose paternity was suspicious? And there seems to have been a Jewish tradition, from at least as early as the second century, which claimed that Jesus was the son of Mary by a Roman soldier named Panthera. Wherever he was born, and whoever his father, Jesus was the family's eldest child and was reared in Nazareth, an obscure village in Galilee in the north of a backwater province which the Romans called Palestine. Galilee was administered by Herod Antipas, a son of Herod the Great and a puppet client of the Romans; and the region was ethnically varied—Jews, Greeks and Syrians, among others. As early as Isaiah 9.1, it's called "Galilee of the Gentiles"; and in Jesus' lifetime, Jews may have been a minority there, though that's far from certain.

Jesus seems to have spent his youth working with his brothers in Joseph's construction business. The Greek word so famously translated *carpenter* can mean, more broadly, a *builder*. One early tradition says that Jesus was the family's ironworker, therefore a blacksmith. We know little about the literacy rates of his time and place (maybe 95 percent were illiterate); but whether he was literate or not, somehow in his youth—oral memorization was a common method— Jesus acquired extensive knowledge of the sacred Hebrew texts, very likely in Aramaic translation since few Jews of his time comprehended much ancient Hebrew (how many contemporary Americans can read Chaucerian English?). He likewise found time to reflect on what he'd learned. The fact that he's sometimes addressed in the Gospels as *Rabbi* may be a further indication of his ability to read.

Given the variety of peoples and languages he likely encountered in early life, Jesus may have known some Greek and Latin; for despite the hegemony of Rome throughout the Mediterranean world, the Koine Greek which Alexander the Great had left behind in his victorious passage three centuries earlier remained the language of commerce and many forms of Roman and puppet administration. For whatever reasons, Jesus left home in early manhood—richly equipped in the traditions of his people—and walked south into the province of Judea. There Jerusalem lay with its splendid Temple, perhaps the most impressive building in the Roman empire, and the Temple's numerous priesthood. In the nearby Jordan River, Jesus accepted a rite of ritual cleansing from an apocalyptic preacher called John the Baptizer (or Baptist or Dipper, one who dips or submerges in water). At that moment of immersion in the Jordan at the hands of John, Jesus experienced a revelation. It may not have been his first, but it seems to have been decisive. It consisted of a conviction that, then and there, the spirit of God descended upon him like a dove; and the voice of God declared that Jesus was his *beloved* or his *only* son (the Greek word can mean either).

After a substantial period of solitary fasting in the Dead Sea desert, accompanied by intense meditation on the meaning of his baptismal experience, Jesus may have followed the Baptist until that fiery critic of Antipas was arrested. Then Jesus returned to Galilee and began circling through the towns and villages of his home district, mostly along the shores of a middle-sized lake which we call the Sea of Galilee. He announced to audiences of generally poor farmers, fishermen, craftsmen and pariahs the coming of something which many Jews had expected for centuries but which Jesus may never have clearly defined, an imminent reality which he called the Reign of God (a more precise translation than the familiar *Kingdom of God*).

Preparation for that coming called for a change of

heart, what Jesus described as a *turn*, an *about-face*; for he may well have thought that the unfolding of God's Reign would occur in a sudden cataclysmic and perhaps violent divine intervention that would separate good from bad in the human race and assign the bad to eternal punishment, the good to eternal reward. The ethic which he soon began to enunciate in his wanderings was an urgent program then for avoiding such a fate and for life in the Reign, should one be sufficiently blessed to survive its awful arrival.

His simultaneous assertion of the love and care of God for even the most insignificant of creatures (he insistently called God *Father*) increasingly clashed with his warnings of a personal doom for wrongdoers. Indeed, from the start of his career, he kept company with the most despised members of his world—the tax collectors whose sticky fingers served both Herod Antipas and themselves, prostitutes, Roman soldiers, even lepers—and he promised them an extraordinary priority in the Father's coming rule. What can the hardworking village plowman or weaver have made of such an apparent contradiction, such an apparent rejection of their hard-won diligence and daily decency? His own family thought him odd at the very least. Mark 3.21 says that they thought him literally "beside himself," which may mean "deranged," therefore "demon-possessed."

Whatever confusions may have been aroused, Jesus was apparently evenhanded in the most impressive of his early actions—the healing of many men, women and children in the throes of diseases and other physical infirmities ranging from skin ailments and seizures to blindness, paralysis and death itself. The public response to his <u>success as a healer</u>—a wonder-worker after all, in the absence of any reliable medical care—was so overwhelming that Mark seems to say that, early on, <u>Jesus was ambivalent about his newly revealed powers</u> and sometimes fled the oppressively hopeful crowds and vanished into the Galilean hills for reflection and prayer.

<u>If he hadn't retreated</u>, in any case, <u>he'd have had few moments</u> indeed <u>in which to form the thoughts that surfaced in his public teaching</u> and, above all, his <u>parables</u>. Was he also considering the possibility of a simple vanishing, a disappearance into some province or whole other country where this alarming new self could recede into the former village craftsman and where something like a normal human life might begin to grow? But could he have thought of settling in distant Gentile country; and could he have stanched, this early, the powers his hands were demonstrating— healing and ease for desperate people?

In his <u>brief span of teaching and healing</u>, Jesus collected a small band of male, and even female, fol-lowers who attended him more closely than the inescapable crowds. His most intimate disciples, a band of twelve men, were remarkably inept and would prove shamefully disloyal to him in his arrest, trial, tor-ture and death. He also soon earned significant ene-mies—both political and religious—who were offended by his apparent arrogation of the right to for-give sin, his other claims of spiritual authority (includ-ing liberties with their notions of Sabbath and dietary law) and his growing popularity with common people.

Mark 3.6 tells us that, almost from the start, the enemies "began conspiring with the Herodians against Him, as to how they might destroy Him."

Yet even those enemies seem not to have questioned his uncanny powers as an exorcist of demons and a healer of diseases and afflictions. An exorcist, after all, might have operated with satanic, rather than godly, power; and his enemies seem to have accused him of demonic relations. None of their charges offended Jesus more. It was tantamount to denying that his powers came from the Holy Spirit, and in Mark 3.29 he called such a denial an eternally unpardonable wrong (the only such definition he gave).

One of the best attested of his sayings is found in Matthew 11 and Luke 7. It's elicited by a question sent him from John the Baptist—"Are You the Expected One, or shall we look for someone else?" I quote Jesus' reply in the more economical, and therefore more striking, version in Luke 7.22–23.

> "Go and report to John what you have seen and heard: the blind receive sight, the lame walk, the lepers are cleansed, and the deaf hear, the dead are raised up, the poor have the gospel preached to them. Blessed is He who does not take offense at Me."

Not only, then, did Jesus affirm the powers of healing which the Gospels report in such brief but compelling scenes; he appears also to have come, perhaps midway through his career, to accept messianic identity. He may well have kept that identity to himself for a considerable while. Then at a critical late moment, in the presence of the Twelve, he accepts his prime disciple Peter's declaration that Jesus is "Messiah, the son of the living God," though he warns Peter sternly to keep that knowledge secret (even the American Standard Translation unfortunately renders the word <u>christos</u> in Matthew 16.16, Mark 8.29 and Luke 9.20 as *Christ* — from the Greek word for <u>anointed</u> — when Peter plainly meant <u>Messiah,</u> from the Hebrew word for <u>anointed</u>. The award of the Greek name *Christ* to Jesus is an act of the later Jesus sect, not of Jesus' contemporaries).

It's unclear what constituted Jesus' full understanding of the identity and role of Messiah. In fact there seems to have been no generally-agreed-upon expectation of the nature of that shadowy and long-postponed figure among Jews of the first century. The prophecy in Micah 5.2 (written in the late eighth century BC) says only that from Bethlehem would come "One who will go forth for Me to be ruler in Israel." Later messianic hopes ranged from a triumphant commander with the supernatural power to expel Roman oppression to a <u>gifted human</u> being who, like earlier Jewish heroes, <u>would revive</u> his people's <u>trust</u> in the only God. In any case, Jesus had begun — perhaps in the desert withdrawal on the heels of his baptismal vision — to believe that he <u>would perform a central role</u> in the Reign of God, the coming of which he felt so hotly. At some point he began to think of himself as the forthcoming proprietor of that new world — a role to which he assigned another pregnant but mysterious title, first used in scripture in Daniel 7.13: *Son of Man*.

No other speaker in the Gospels called Jesus that, and he never explained its meaning for him.

Eventually Jesus was ready to share his conviction; and he led an especially close group of three disciples up a mountain—probably Mount Hermon, well to the north of Galilee—and there, in an inexplicable moment, the three disciples were convinced that he was changed in shape before them and that they heard a voice, which they took to be God's, declaring Jesus to be his beloved son. They also saw, standing beside him on the mountain, Moses and Elijah—two distant but central figures in the Jewish hope for deliverance from long bondage to other powers. Soon after that moment of transfiguration, Jesus began to tell all his disciples he must die as "a ransom for many."

There are memorable passages in Isaiah, which may lie behind Jesus' growing sense of a sacrificial destiny for himself. This Son of God and Son of Man would end his earthly life as a Messiah who

> . . . was pierced through for our transgres-
>   sions,
> He was crushed for our iniquities;
> The chastening for our well-being fell upon
>   Him.
> And by His scourging we are healed.
>   Isaiah 53.5

The fact that none of the Gospels gives the least hint that Jesus made these self-discoveries with the counsel of any other human being only adds weight to a reader's sense of his eventual solitude and fear, then terror and abandonment. Can this potent yet poetic young man have so much as begun to foresee the price he was volunteering to pay for the rescue he meant to offer humankind? Had he made some appalling mistake, hearing voices that seemed to come from God, when perhaps his enemies were right? Perhaps, after all, he'd been no more than a po-faced pawn of the Prince of Lies; and every apparent good deed he'd done was empowered by Satan.

In the spring of about the year 30, Jesus led his followers south toward Jerusalem, the nexus of his people's faith, where the spirit of God Himself had dwelt in the Temple built by David's son, King Solomon, and then in the process of a magnificent restoration begun by Herod the Great. Jesus' reasons for approaching the heart of a potentially lethal opposition are not clear. Mark, Matthew and Luke imply that he went there in a conscious effort to seek a sacrificial death for what he calls in Mark 10.45 "a ransom for many."

Albert Schweitzer, the most eloquent and imposing of modern New Testament scholars, asserted in his *Quest of the Historical Jesus* that Jesus, baffled that the Reign of God had not arrived as he expected, traveled to Jerusalem in the hope of somehow triggering that apocalypse. Perhaps by hurling his own life into the teeth of his enemies, he could speed his hope—and his own transcendent role—onward. (Schweitzer's claim, made in 1906, has been fiercely debated ever since. Many older British scholars and the majority of the Jesus Seminar, for instance, reject the possibility that Jesus was a literal apocalypticist—and one who was therefore wrong—but the force of Schweitzer's claim, and the burden of evidence in New Testament documents, has returned to convince many current scholars.)

It was the time of the spring Passover feast; and Jesus arranged to enter the teeming city on ass back, surrounded with a cheering crowd. By that seemingly unremarkable act, he now publicly claimed messianic status—a prophecy in Zechariah 9.9 was understood as foretelling such an entry. Since the arrival failed to provoke immediate retaliation by the Romans or his own people's Temple authorities, perhaps the demonstration was small and unspectacular. In the absence of civil restraint, during the next few days Jesus engaged in some form of disorderly interruption of commerce within the precincts of the Temple. He cried out that he was purifying the holy place from what he called *bandits*, but the degree of violence involved in the episode is no longer certain. It may have involved little more than overturning a few moneychangers' tables and disturbing a few sacrificial animals.

Whatever the degree of his opposition to priestly authority, again the action met with no immediate repression. Still unopposed, Jesus proceeded to teach in the broad open Temple courts, debating peacefully with other teachers and lawyers. But the High Priest and the Sanhedrin, his council of advisors—all of them in subordinate power at the tolerance of the Roman governor of Judea—were watching intently, concerned that Jesus' escalating symbolic acts and claims would bring down even more severe imperial repression. The Roman authorities were likewise especially watchful during festival time in a city much given to rebellious outbursts. No doubt their guards and agents were filing reports and caressing their weapons, if no more than cudgels.

For an uncertain combination of offenses then — and in expectation of whatever retaliation — toward the end of Passover, Jesus bade farewell to his disciples in a nighttime meal that, regardless of its date, served for him as the Passover observance and which he ended with a laconic but so-far-unforgettable redefinition of the meaning of bread and wine. Paul's account of the moment, in 1 Corinthians 11.23–25, is some ten years older even than Mark's.

> . . . the Lord Jesus in the night in which He was betrayed took bread; and when He had given thanks, He broke it and said, "This is My body, which is for you; do this in remembrance of Me." In the same way He took the cup also after supper, saying, "This cup is the new covenant in My blood; do this, as often as you drink it, in remembrance of Me."

When he and the disciples had sung the appropriate hymn, Jesus led them to a garden in the valley just east of the Temple; and in an anguished time of prayer (Mark 14.33 says he "began to be very distressed and troubled"), he addressed God in the most intimate of Aramaic words for *father* — *abba* — and he begged his Father to spare him the sacrificial fate which he'd courted. That hour of terror, through which even his innermost group of disciples drowsed, was ended by no act of angelic rescue nor the thunderous advent of the

Reign but by the sudden arrival of a cohort of Temple police.

They'd been brought to the spot by Judas Iscariot, one of the Twelve. For his own never-explained reasons, Judas had sold Jesus' nocturnal whereabouts to the Temple authorities. Jesus' male followers bolted unceremoniously and abandoned this man who'd perhaps led them to expect places in the Reign of God but delivered only humiliation. Peter and an unnamed companion lurked nearby till Peter at last denied all knowledge of Jesus for the third time and fled in shame. Only a few immovable women and one "disciple whom Jesus loved" (otherwise unnamed in the Gospel of John) would stay loyal through the coming ordeal.

Swiftly questioned by the Sanhedrin, Jesus again asserted his identity as Messiah. He may also have claimed to be the Son of Man, who would come

> "sitting at the right hand of Power, and
> coming with the clouds of heaven."
>   Mark 14.62

The understandably alarmed Sanhedrin condemned him worthy of death — they appear not to have had the right of capital punishment — and delivered him next morning to the Roman prefect Pilate with the assertion that Jesus had claimed to be "King of the Jews."

Pilate was then resident in Jerusalem to oversee the dangers of Passover disorder. Few claims could have more readily seized Pilate's attention and left him readier to act swiftly and decisively. After a cursory interrogation, the prefect — who would soon be recalled by the emperor for excessive administrative harshness in other matters—sentenced the would-be troublemaker to death by crucifixion. And on the eve of the sabbath, the sentence was carried out by Roman soldiers (the date was probably 7 April in the year 30). After some six hours Jesus died, sooner than might have been expected in a uniquely gruesome procedure, designed to prolong the agony of the crucified. His final words in Matthew 27 and Mark 15—"My God, My God, why have You forsaken Me?"—are the opening words of Psalm 22, a prolonged lament which ends less desperately than it begins. It seems unlikely however that a man at the end of six hours nailed to a cross, naked in the presence of his taunting enemies, would have commenced the recitation of a longish poem in the hopes of reaching its serene concluding lines. In fact, the words are so desolate that only two Gospels report them as Jesus' last.

The chance that Jesus died in despair of the love of God—and in the profoundest bafflement of his hopes of commanding God's kingdom—is a chance, even a likelihood, that seems all but inescapable. Whatever his meaning in that exhausted final moment, God's Reign had not arrived as Jesus expected—or hoped. The day of his death was declining toward sunset. The sabbath was impending, and the Romans had acceded to Jewish sensitivities toward the exposure of dying criminals on the sabbath. So Pilate permitted the swift burial of Jesus' corpse in a tomb hewn from live rock and owned by Joseph of Arimathea, a member of the Sanhedrin who had some sympathy with Jesus' teaching and offered his own new sepulchre.

Two days after the burial, visiting Jesus' tomb on Sunday at dawn in hopes of completing their anointment of the corpse, a few of the loyal women discovered that the large stone which had closed the mouth of the tomb had been rolled away; and the corpse was gone. There they—or perhaps only Mary of Magdala—experienced a first encounter with the risen Jesus. They reported their experience to the quailing men; and despite the fact that women were considered unreliable witnesses in Jewish courts, many of the early historians of Jesus' life did not conceal the fact that the first witnesses of the resurrection were women, unaccompanied by men.

Soon after the women's discovery, various of his followers—including the uncomprehending cowards who'd deserted him—underwent experiences which they believed to be meetings with a Jesus risen from the dead and transformed in some inexplicable but slowly recognizable, palpable and speaking form. Again, the nature of these meetings cannot be recovered. Were they visionary or had Jesus not died on the cross, and fraud was perpetrated? Or did the appearances represent an entirely supernatural victory over death? The Gospels, and the great majority of the subsequent Jesus sect, insist upon the latter possibility.

Whatever the experiences, their effects were so intense as to galvanize the nucleus of eleven surviving disciples—Judas soon killed himself—and a few hundred other followers into a group which began, with unquenchable fervor and eloquence in the face of murderous opposition, to spread the news of Jesus' conquest of mortality. In the Book of Acts 1.3, Luke says that Jesus' appearances continued for forty days, though Paul considered his own vision of Jesus some few years later to be the last known manifestation. However long they lasted and whatever their nature—the appearances narrated in the Gospels range from unspectacular to awesome yet credible—these encounters embodied a victory hoped for by most human beings in all known ages: *we do not need to die.*

Two hundred and eighty-two years later, the witnesses and their successive generations of pupils had traveled so widely with their good news and succeeded so well with their eloquence that in 312 the Emperor Constantine himself was converted to faith in the enduring power of Jesus; and he declared the despised sect—one which many prior emperors had attempted to exterminate—a legitimate religion. Then with astonishing speed, the Jesus sect proceeded to become the triumphal religious and political institution of the Roman empire and its national successors in Europe and eventually the world.

2. A CROWD OF DISSONANT VOICES

That sketch of a career and its aftermath is—as I warned—subject to endless questions and objections, including flat refusal from all sides; but again, more than a century of probing into the life of Jesus by scholars from a wide spectrum of persuasions seems to me to have established some such scaffolding for any but the most constitutionally skeptical or hypercautious or those adamantly opposed to any suggestion that violates the boundaries of nineteenth-century science (not at all incidentally, it's worth adding here that almost no scholar who's carefully investigated the evidence has doubted Jesus' existence in history). My summary is at least a narrative made from our only prior records, a story that proceeds with the expected logic of lifelike human accounts—and one which, furthermore, hews as closely as possible to the narrative progression of the oldest Gospel, Mark. Yet anyone who so much as nears the suggestion of writing a life of Jesus must notify his readers that there are contemporary scholars—some of whom are respectable students and some of whom count themselves Christians—who believe that the Gospels present us with very little, if any, reliable information about the central figure of their story.

It's necessary to add here that no scholars are more subject to the ceaseless qualms of the overwhelmed student than those who focus on the life of Jesus. A number of them stand among the most distinguished students of any of the ancient major disciplines, yielding to none in the breadth and depth of their pursuits and reflections; but they share a danger unique to their subject. Most of them entered their discipline as believing Christians; and however their studies ultimately affect their faith, they're uniquely prone— once they've earned their scholarly credentials—to shoot themselves in the foot when confronted with evidence that would satisfy almost any other historian of ancient life.

Contemporary students of Greek and Roman history, for instance, draw sane conclusions from partial evidence which New Testament scholars are loath to draw from evidence that's often at least as credible. As a single example I'd point to an increasing scholarly reluctance to acknowledge that the return of Jesus from the dead, whether in some still inexplicable corporeal form or a repeated visionary one, is a firmly attested fact. Yet no moment in recorded history is the subject of more contention. Indeed it's been a truism of New Testament scholarship for at least half a century now that the resurrection cannot be discussed as a historical event because sufficient evidence does not exist. Who, though, questions that Socrates of Athens taught in a quizzical manner; that Alexander the Great was eventually an alcoholic or that the Emperor Caligula was barking mad? For which of those items do we have firmer historical evidence than for Jesus' potent survival—in some uniquely perceptible form—of death? Admittedly, no one known to me presently worships any of those three men; but surely the question has some force.

What my sketch of Jesus' career most glaringly omits—apart from any discussion of the more extraordinary healings and nature miracles recounted in the Gospels—is any firm assertion about the core of his teaching and any attempt to define his full identity (I have nothing to add to the stacks of controversy on those subjects, though I've written elsewhere of my own experience with the healing power of Jesus*).

---

*In my poem "Vision" (*Collected Poems*); my account of a crippling battle with cancer of the spinal cord, *A Whole New Life*; and in *Letter to a Man in the Fire* (all Scribner). The poem "Vision" is included, as an appendix, at the end of this volume.

Those two questions and their related concerns will be central for the remainder of this book. Again, why did he insist—or demonstrate in silent actions—that his ethic was of greater weight than that of any other rabbi or of the Law itself, or did he make any such assertion? What kinds of lives did he demand of his followers (or commend to them); and if he expected the imminent end of the world around him, why did he propose what seems to be an ethic meant for long and busy human existences? Finally who did he claim he was, and who did his pupils consider him to be in the months before his death?

Despite two millennia of study, speculation, worship and atrociously bloody dispute, those central questions remain so large that they're almost surely unanswerable except by commitments of a faith that seems reckless to most onlookers—those same leaps which have powered the best and worst things done in Jesus' name. Such hurdles, however invisible and silent they may be, seem harder than ever for thoughtful men and women to make, especially those reared in families with no enacted religious traditions and educated in systems which fail to provide even a minimal awareness of the narrative and moral content of a culture's founding religions.

That second question—who *was* Jesus?—is one with which I won't be as heavily concerned here as the first. A focus on at least a few aspects of his ethical teaching is my main concern, and for a start I'd suggest that any reader who desires a firmer knowledge of Jesus' ethical teaching could proceed most effectively by acquiring one of those easily available and surprisingly instructive copies of the Gospels in which the words of Jesus are printed in red ink to distinguish them from the black-ink prose of the evangelists. Even a rapid survey of the red ink will establish at least two things. First, virtually everything in red is intellectually and rhetorically of greater interest than everything in black. And second, despite voluminous efforts by centuries of theologians to iron out apparent contradictions in Jesus' teaching, there are troubling—indeed, daunting—disparities, both explicit and implicit, in the teaching reported by our four witnesses: Mark, Matthew, Luke and John.*

---

*Despite recent claims by some scholars, the sayings of Jesus reported in the first- or second-century *Gospel of Thomas* (discovered in Egypt in 1945) hardly affect our sense of Jesus' meaning. A few of them provide moments of a poetry as striking as any in the canonical sayings, but none of the 114 sayings appreciably alters our understanding of the man's work. The other surviving New Testament apocrypha, which come almost surely from the second and third centuries, are sadly fragmentary, though again there are a few striking flashes of an eloquence that may derive from Jesus himself. To give two examples from *Thomas*—

"Do not tell lies, and do not do what you hate, for all things are plain in the sight of heaven."

"It is I who am the light which is above them all. It is I who am the all. From me did the all come forth, and unto me did the all extend. Split a piece of wood, and I am there. Lift up the stone, and you will find me there."

(translated by Thomas O. Lambdin)

Whether some of the other fragments suggest the degree to which the four canonical Gospels represent a severe censoring, by early Christians, of a historically more libertarian Jesus is a matter which may be reviewed in Elaine Pagels's *The Gnostic Gospels* (Random House).

To note a single contradiction among many, on numerous occasions Jesus appears to ignore—if not violate—important aspects of the Mosaic Law which was so deeply bred in his bones. Yet in Matthew 5.17 he says "Do not think that I've come to abolish the Law or the Prophets; I did not come to abolish but to fulfill" (to be sure, we no longer know what Jesus meant by the word *fulfill*; I might claim, quite cogently, that I was fulfilling the intent of a certain law by violating it—the entire philosophy of civil disobedience, for instance, arises from such claims).

And most puzzling of all, especially for those who prefer to think of Jesus as unfailingly merciful in his dealings with others, is the greatest paradox he offers— he steadily displayed a strong personal tolerance of sinners proscribed by the Law and, right through the day of his ghastly death (according to the Gospels of Luke and John), he attempted to rely upon what he had insisted was the boundlessly loving nature of God. He had earlier warned, however—especially in the Gospel of Matthew—of the fiercely vindictive intent of that same Father upon all those who violate His commands.

The mystery embodied in that troubling—and, for many, terrifying—paradox has long been apparent to watchful readers of the Gospels and those other documents which derive from Jesus' first-century followers, the authors of the remaining texts which comprise the New Testament. For more than a century now, scholars have labored to classify and comprehend the sayings of Jesus and to segregate from their midst those sayings which may be outright creations of his earliest followers or messages those followers claimed, earnestly or in fraud, to have received from the risen Jesus or in later visions of him. A few of the contradictory or apparently uncharacteristic sayings may be the result of such origins. Unless a trove of relevant manuscripts should be unearthed — and such a discovery is by no means impossible — we'll never know.

The most recent major skirmish in the textual wars came in the 1990s when a group calling itself the Jesus Seminar won the publicity it so avidly sought by announcing that fewer than 20 percent of the canonically reported sayings of Jesus were ever spoken by him. A sprinkling of the livelier and more thoroughly trained members of the Seminar have asked useful questions and offered provocative answers; but their joint attempt at devastating the body of Jesus' sayings, and the historical content of the Gospels, was met with the combination of popular consternation and mainline scholarly amusement that it deserved.

An even younger generation of scholars has begun to approach the Gospel record with the two-handed engine of critical theory and its frequently relentless political agendas. *Critical theory* is a power tool, initially built by American literary scholars with parts from French philosophy, anthropology and psychoanalytic speculation; and like a good many such hybrid engines, it's capable of so thoroughly clouding the user's only means of communicating his findings — which is in sentences composed of words — that he mauls himself at least as often as he usefully lays bare the spine of his subject (and men are by no means the only mauled users).

Some of the youngest theorists, especially those most concerned with Gospel narrative, are more alert to the complexities of understanding and conjecture laid down in centuries of prior patient study. Many of the younger students, however, are capable of a breathtakingly wholesale refusal to credit vitally important cultural matters that they cannot themselves have experienced—a refusal that's at least as broad-stroked and groundlessly destructive in intent as that of the Jesus Seminar. Those crucial ignored realities include such matters as the astonishing durability of certain kinds of human memory and the dogged persistence of oral narrative in preserving significant stretches of reliable history, especially when those memories were formed in cultures conditioned to exactly such forms of preservation.

In short then, any reader in hope of a patch of firm ground in the presently seismic country of Jesus scholarship (and the subject has been in a state of heavy tremor since the mid–nineteenth century) is likely to feel that the land will never sit still again. Perhaps it won't; there's never a guarantee that any form of knowledge will freeze before our eyes—what we've relied on as "science" for at least a century is in even greater flux than Jesus studies. Yet all such scholarly tilting—whether biographical, textual or theological— has done little to discourage the at-least-nominal faith, or the daily behavior, of nearly two billion human beings. Even at a time of resurgent fundamentalist Islam in many countries, Christianity remains by some distance the most populous religion on Earth and is reportedly gaining quantities of new adherents in the southern hemisphere. In the United States today, 82 percent of the population declares itself to be Christian. (I reiterate the size of Christianity for two reasons. First, the moral prescriptions and compulsions of the religion are my chief concern here; and the diversity of Christian ethical practices is startling. Second, when I've recently asked friends their estimate of the world's largest religion, most of them have named either Islam or Hinduism.)

If daily experience of our neighbors compels us to grant that a number of those claimants are Christian through family habit alone and have no special knowledge of the principles of a particular church, much less the deducible teachings of Jesus, then close observation of the American Christian community alone — wildly diverse as it is — will also conclude that a substantial share of the Christian majority of men and women is more devoted to some personal concept of the figure of Jesus, Jesus as an unnervingly live being, than to any particular set of dogmas and rules.

Those degrees of private devotion begin perhaps in the driver who sports, with no humorous intent, a bumper sticker saying "Jesus Is My Best Friend" or even the ambivalent "Honk If You Love Jesus" (a friend reports a recent sighting of "Honk If You *Are* Jesus"). And the unmistakable signs of private involvement proceed through the emotions of churchgoing individuals who try hard to pursue the life of active charity, tolerance and mercy which they believe Jesus required them to lead. Devotion may even move onward to those rare clerics and the generally secret civilians whose dedication to the example of the earthly Jesus impels them toward an emulation of the glorified Son of God on the Mount of Transfiguration, the tormented man in the Garden of Gethsemane and the agonized sacrificial victim on Golgotha.

A few evenings ago I watched, again, at a distance the stumbling form of someone I've glimpsed at intervals for several years. The person is highly respected yet appears to be nearing death from chosen starvation (at closer range on other occasions, I can count each bone that lies behind the face). As I watched, the person was taking sips of water from a bottle and spitting them out—no swallowing. I'm told that the person has chosen a life of strict Christian asceticism and accepts little nourishment but the communion wafer. Yet no close friend of the person with whom I've spoken seems to doubt the sincerity of the person's choice. The history of ancient and medieval Christianity offers more than one parallel to such imponderable devotion to the suffering Jesus, but a contemporary example is rare.

The figure of Jesus, in all the avatars deducible from the Gospels and the numerous other forms pressed upon him by his followers, has been so deeply engrained in our national psyche from the start of European settlement here; and his presence continues to remain central in the feelings of so many million Americans, that it's critically important to recall how many people find his looming presence objectionable or far worse. Those reactions may come from the increasingly large number of American Muslims for whom Jesus is an acknowledged prophet of Islam, worthy of attention and respect but not of worship. They may come from American Jews who have never seen Jesus as the anointed Messiah much less as an earthly incarnation of God himself. They likewise come from atheists, agnostics, Unitarians, a good many other honest dissenters and from those silent guests in our midst who move in disguise with the burning hope of destroying as many as possible of the citizens of a society which has grown with Christian banners streaming but has so often brutally ignored the misery of millions, domestic and foreign.

I myself had two recent experiences with complex responses on the part of intelligent Americans to the figure of Jesus. In 1997 I received a letter from a young stranger, who was dying of pancreatic cancer. He asked me to answer two questions for him—does God exist and does He care? Though I tracked the young man down by phone and talked with him at some length (he was four hundred miles away), he died before I could finish the response I promised. Still I completed a full reply—I say *reply* because I was surely not one who could *answer* the outsized challenge he set me—and I published it two years later in a volume called *Letter to a Man in the Fire*.

The American poet Edward Hirsch reviewed the book in the *New York Times Book Review*. Hirsch had read my text sympathetically but only to a point. I was more surprised than I should have been, no doubt, by one of his sentences. He said "As a Jew, I simply don't believe the same things the author does—in a way, Jesus interposes himself between this book and me— and I find myself wrestling with the faith of a man whose writings I greatly appreciate but whose belief system seems distant and even alien to me." What surprised me in Hirsch's patently honest remark was the realization that a man of his cultural and historical awareness was nonetheless prepared to impute to the figure of Jesus the ceaseless wrongs of Jesus' followers, not the man himself. A contemporary American poet of considerable achievement, which Hirsch is, had declared himself incapable of studying the record and the full import of an ancient teacher who arose, after all, from the religious tradition of his own forebears and died in their faith (Jesus' final words from the cross, in all the Gospels, reveal no rejection of the faith of his lifetime). That refusal continues to amaze me.

A peculiarly polar experience arose not many months later when I was asked by *Time* magazine to write a cover story about Jesus for one of their end-of-millennium issues. I accepted the invitation and submitted a lengthy essay. The editor with whom I worked was a helpful Asian American. As my essay proceeded through the immense machinery of *Time's* various departments, I received numerous edits and proofs; and I began to notice that one of my sentences, a sentence of great importance to me, disappeared each time I resubmitted it. On its third disappearance, I asked my editor why; and he told me that his own superior—the then managing editor of the magazine, whose name at least implied an eastern European Jewish heritage—repeatedly cut it.

At that point I said to my editor "Tell your managing editor that the sentence in question is intended for his great-grandfather." Thereafter the disappearing

sentence silently resurfaced and appeared in my essay
as it ran in *Time* on 6 December 1999. It follows,
toward the end of the essay, upon my dissenting from
the uses made of what is called the Great Commission
of Jesus, that saying at the very end of the Gospel of
Matthew, which I've already noted—

> "Go therefore and make disciples of all
> nations, baptizing them in the name of the
> Father, the Son, and the Holy Spirit."

My essay then added "Given the gleaming confidence
of those words, and in light of the ghastly failures of
Jesus' followers, that last command goes on con-
tributing heavily to the evils of national and religious
warfare, institutional and individual hatred, imperialism and enslavement—and all in the name of a
teacher who, to our knowledge, never refused a single
person who approached him honestly." I've still never
communicated with that managing editor, and I have
no certainty of his great-grandfather's origins or fate,
but I'm grateful that the sentence appeared in so
widely read a journal as *Time*. No honest witness of
world history could hope for less.

While students of the life and work of Jesus can
hardly hope to convey their best sense of his meaning
to all his objectors, contemporary scholarship has
achieved at least one important form of truth-telling in
the interests of partial reparation to a people who've
suffered unspeakably at the hands of Jesus' followers.
For the major achievement of the past five decades of
New Testament scholarship has been a clarification—

or more accurately, the first broad-scaled recovery in almost two millennia—of the central fact of the Jewishness of Jesus, of all his earliest pupils and of at least the first generation of those who carried the news of his resurrection and what they took to be his significance beyond the boundaries of Palestine.

Recent scholarship, conducted by both Gentiles and Jews, has made it clear that Jesus lived, taught and died as a Jew who observed the Law of his people. Further, it seems entirely likely that—before his death— he never envisioned a new sect founded in his own name, nor did his immediate disciples. The fact that the Aramaic word by which Jesus described his followers (perhaps *qahal*, meaning *community* or *gathering*) and its Greek translation *ekklesia* (meaning, likewise, *group* or *assembly*) are almost always translated *church*, with all that word's institutional connotations, is a grave misrepresentation.

3. HIS NEWS

Given that even those twenty-first-century persons who cannot think of him as divine often revere him as an ethical teacher, it's worth noting that a number of well-informed scholars of both Judaism and the words of Jesus have found little in his ethical teaching which can't be paralleled in earlier Jewish law and rabbinical tradition (here it may be important to recall that only Luke, of the four Gospel-writers, seems to have been a Gentile). The originality of his ethic remains under considerable discussion, though few deny Jesus' powers of eloquence, concision and the probing and often witty village and agrarian imagination from which he generated his strikingly new metaphors.

His parables, though built around principles implicit in Judaism, are a distinctive and (in his hands) often original means of teaching, both in the freshness of their literary form and their implications. And they're ample enough in their embrace to include a pleasing and useful array of characters—from rich men of brunt (even brute) power and sleek religious bureaucrats downward through common men and women of average decency and those whom many of his hearers despised as the scum of their world. The plain but enormous fact that Jesus thought, and cared enough, about such wide armfuls of human beings that his mind—early on—began to generate such a large battery of realistic stories (none of them is a fantasy, and almost none is an allegory) is among the strongest signs that distinguish him from his apocalyptic forebear, John the Baptist, and his more scornful contemporaries in the ranks of religious power—the teachers, lawyers and rulers whom the Gospels portray as his enemies.

In the little matter that survives, in text or tradition, from those first-century teachers and bureaucrats, Jesus' parables—however they may have been revised by his early followers—show him to be in unique possession of a humane embrace that yearns toward a renewal of the late prophetic hope of God's eternal care for each human life and the salvation He may intend for each of them, Jew or Gentile. That piercing hope illuminates the vision of Jesus as steadily as it does that of his most eloquent modern disciple, Dostoevsky—so steadily that a contemporary student may well take it for Jesus' central passion.

But in light of the contention that his ethical teaching is largely an echo of predecessors in his own religious tradition, it's pertinent to wonder who—among the moral teachers on whom enduring religions are founded—is largely original. What is there in the teachings of the Buddha and Muhammad, for instance, which cannot be found—implicitly at least—in the work of earlier teachers to whom they may have had access? In those two cases I'm unqualified to answer with any degree of confidence, but I wouldn't be surprised if the answer suggested that the motor power of each of those teachers lay primarily in the experiences of the sudden and private revelation or enlightenment which each of them reported. Certainly the Buddha's claim of attaining *nirvana* with its attendant release from human desire and the resulting access to a serene new perspective, and Muhammad's receipt of the Koran from Allah's dictation were experiences of large and ongoing import for the life of humankind.

Nowhere in the Gospels, however—nor indeed in the early Christian apocryphal writings known to me—does Jesus himself quite describe such an exclusive personal revelation. In Matthew 11.27 he may hint at such a gift.

> "All things have been handed over to Me by
> My Father; and no one knows the Son except
> the Father; nor does anyone know the Father

except the Son, and anyone to whom the Son wills to reveal Him."

And in John 14.6, shortly before his arrest, he delivers to the disciples at their last supper the most exclusionary of all his sayings.

"I am the way and the truth and the life; no one comes to the Father but through Me."

Soon thereafter he says

"The words that I say to you I do not speak on My own initiative, but the Father abiding in Me does His works."

Nowhere in John, however, does Jesus himself reveal the source of his self-certainty; that's conveyed directly by the author to the reader in the first chapter of the Gospel when Jesus is forthrightly presented as the Word of God—in fact as God. Even the voice of God which Jesus hears at the moment of his baptism in Mark 1 (and again in Mark's mysterious transfiguration scene) is reported by the author, not by Jesus himself, though it may be reasonably argued that Jesus would have described the baptismal experience to his pupils and that they would have transmitted it to their successors. Three of the pupils were, however, present at the transfiguration on the mountain; and they heard God's voice calling Jesus his Son. Luke 9.31 says that, during that same event, the figures of Moses and Elijah discussed with him the events of his coming *departure*. So we're left to wonder whether the wisdom which Jesus transmits in his teaching, and his certainty of the imminence of God's kingdom, were deduced in his early youth primarily from his study of scripture and his own observation of the world or whether he was vouchsafed some further knowledge in private communications from God — revelations which he may never have described to any of his pupils.

If Jesus could be shown to have originated little as an ethical teacher, a majority of modern Christians would respond with a shrug. What's most compelling for them — what most of them see as unique in his meaning — is not his ethic, his rhetoric (magnetic as it is in both its welcoming and frightening phases), his healings and broad compassion, but the simple fact of his resurrection. And that quiet triumph over death — all the Gospel accounts of the appearances are remarkable for their implicit silence: no trumpets or gongs, no angel hymns, no screams of recognition — is the ultimate validation of Jesus' life and death, even if we conclude (as many do not) that he was simply wrong about the nearness of the Reign. His return from death has likewise been seen by his followers, ever since, as a pledge that God offers eternal life to those who believe that Jesus was uniquely His Son and who follow his example — the full meaning of *follow* is of course the largest, and generally most defeating, riddle Christians face. Equally, his resurrection is the ultimate validation of his ethic. Shouldn't one give unusually serious attention to obeying the commands, the advice, of any such man?

Despite its apparent preposterousness, the enduring belief in Jesus' palpable resurrection from death is not without arresting first-century evidence. I've already noted that the strongest evidence is the otherwise inexplicable reversal which his cowardly pupils underwent soon after his death, a reversal which E. P. Sanders, one of the most formidably learned students of Jesus' life, describes in his judicious *Historical Figure of Jesus*.

> Finally we know that after his death his followers experienced what they described as the "resurrection": the appearance of a living but transformed person who had actually died. They believed this, they lived it, and they died for it.

My friend Moody Smith, a great scholar of the Gospel of John (among numerous other distinctions), has recently said in a note to me,

> A question that I've found useful is: "Did the resurrection happen to Jesus himself or to the disciples?" One could say, "The disciples," but if the disciples didn't believe it happened to Jesus they wouldn't have been interested.

It would be possible of course to suggest that the disciples might, momentarily at least, have been interested in the fame, the power or even the financial gain they could win as firsthand witnesses and spiritual heirs of a risen master. But almost all the Twelve drop from the sight of history immediately after Jesus' arrest; and those who survived to acquire later attention—above all, Peter, James the son of Zebedee, and Jesus' brother James (not one of the Twelve)—were eventually killed for their lifelong witness to the raising of Jesus.

Any survey of evidence for the resurrection must soon contend with the figure of Paul or Saul. Saul of Tarsus—a tentmaker, a Pharisee* and a devoted student of the Law—was changed from a fierce pursuer of the Jesus sect into one of the most impelled early Christians when he received what he said was Jesus' last resurrection appearance. Thereafter he changed his name to Paul (though Paul may have been his accustomed earlier Roman name), spent his remaining thirty-odd years in tireless missionary journeys round the Mediterranean basin, was ultimately executed under the Emperor Nero in Rome in the early to mid sixties AD and endures as the most influential of Western theologians. The very cornerstone of Paul's theology, as it was the fuel of his matchless energy, was a confidence that Jesus of Nazareth actually died and was actually raised from the dead by the hand of God—an indubitable presence, visible in an excess

*The Pharisees, whom the Gospels almost surely over-emphasize as Jesus' chief opponents, were a party of devoted students and servants of the Law. They differed from the high-priestly party, the Sadducees, primarily in the Pharisees' insistence that the tradition of oral interpretation, which had grown to surround the written Law, was worthy of intense study and binding respect. In the lifetime of Jesus, the Pharisees were likely the most liberal of important religious and political groups in Judaic Palestine.

of light (Jesus' appearance to Paul was apparently obscured by literally blinding light).

In the fifteenth chapter of his first Letter to the Corinthians—written some twenty years after Jesus' death and reporting an already established tradition received by Paul within five years of the crucifixion— Paul enumerates the persons who experienced the risen Jesus, though in typical Pauline fashion, he omits the absolute first appearance to the women at the tomb. And it's also in 1 Corinthians 15.14 that Paul makes a flat assertion which anyone who claims to be a Christian must somehow accommodate.

> . . . and if Christ has not been raised, then our preaching is vain, your faith also is vain.

Since Saul of Tarsus first entered the Jesus sect and began so busily to transform it, many followers of Jesus have had grave problems with more than one aspect of Paul's voluble teaching. A great many have even seen Saul/Paul as the inventor of what we presently call Christianity, a religion designed (consciously or unconsciously, they say) to be a fatal enemy of the teaching and compassionate life of Jesus of Nazareth. For all the sublimity of his hymn to love in 1 Corinthians 13 and scattered other passages of a likable gratitude and tenderness, Paul was also a ferocious hater, a brilliant but often obscure and self-contradictory thinker, a man in agonized ambivalence as to whether or not a belief in Jesus' Sonship had superseded the Mosaic Law, an apparent despiser of most forms of sexual expression and one who did not share his master's interest in women. Despite all reservations about Paul, however—and some of them are enduringly powerful—no one can deny at least two facts.

First is the reality that first- and second-generation Christianity comprised a tiny splinter Jewish sect which almost certainly would not have survived to become a world religion without the driving force of intellect, language and physical endurance compacted in the small and wiry baldheaded body of Paul.* The second undeniable reality is the intensity of Paul's certainty that Jesus of Nazareth rose from the dead and appeared to him, astoundingly and decisively. That certainty was so unshakable that, because of it, he was executed (Roman tradition says he was beheaded). To be sure, such a personal conviction and martyrdom is, in itself, proof of nothing. Hundreds of thousands

---

*My description derives from the second-century apocryphal *Acts of Paul*. There, Paul is described as

> according to 'Titus' description . . . a man small of stature, with a bald head and crooked legs, in a good state of body, with eyebrows meeting and nose somewhat hooked, full of friendliness; for now he appeared like a man, and now he had the face of an angel.
> [translated by R. McL. Wilson in Hennecke and Schneemelcher, *New Testament Apocrypha*, III, pp. 353–54 (Westminster)]

While it's not known who wrote the *Acts of Paul*, the author appears to have had access to several possibly reliable traditions. In any case, this description is borne out in many of the oldest portraits of Paul. It's impossible to say, however, whether that early image relies on the *Acts of Paul*. In any case, the description has seemed so perfect a fit for the man deducible from the Acts of the Apostles and from Paul's letters that it's become a virtually canonical picture.

of human beings have flung themselves onto violent death in support of beliefs (theological, philosophical and political) that are long-forgotten, discredited or even lunatic. Yet the record of centuries of martyred believers in the ongoing and redeeming power of the man Jesus remains intellectually arresting, at least, and emotionally impressive as models in the lives of many contemporary men and women.

4. A QUESTION MORE LIKELY THAN IT LOOKS

Among recent reflections of that power is a development in American Christianity that deserves more serious attention than it's received. It's occurred in a movement that flies the banner WWJD—*What Would Jesus Do?* When I first encountered the phrase, and its brush-fire popularity in certain youth circles, I remember thinking at once "Does anyone ever say 'What would Buddha do or Muhammad or Zoroaster or Confucius?'"* With that I retired my curiosity, and it's only recently that I've looked more closely into the WWJD phenomenon. As I suspected, its origins are peculiarly American. Perhaps because of the brevity of our history as a nation, Americans have an unusual ability to engage in imaginary relations with dead but

*Shortly after writing this sentence, I was downing an espresso at my local bookstore when I glanced at a rack ten yards ahead and saw a book I should have known existed—*What Would Buddha Do?* And on a recent return visit, I chanced upon, of course, *What Would Jesus Eat?*

emblematic men and women. Do any French natives, for instance, now feel about Charlemagne or Joan of Arc the way some young—and older—Americans demonstrably feel about, say, Abraham Lincoln, Robert E. Lee, Sitting Bull or Sojourner Truth?

The beginnings of the WWJD movement are remindful of that imaginative ability. It was sparked in 1989 by a youth leader at the Calvary Reformed Church in Holland, Michigan. She'd read a once popular American novel called *In His Steps*, had gleaned from it the "What Would Jesus Do?" principle; and she introduced it to her young charges as a guide for moral choice. They took to the challenge, and word of their enthusiasm spread rapidly through the United States and Europe.

Quite apart from any merits inherent in such a baldly worded question, a prowler of the Internet can quickly learn what an industry was promptly generated by the phrase. A horde of books, audiotapes and calendars was published; conferences were held, summer camps were organized, T-shirts were sold and worn; but the most visible of all external signs were the notorious WWJD bracelets, available at retail outlets and distributed free at concerts by a popular band called 'NSYNC. It comes as no surprise, however, to learn from further entries on the Internet that the phenomenon was primarily an enthusiasm of the nineties and that it may now be receding.

Meanwhile, it would be easy enough to grin at the flurry of superficial interest in an ancient teacher's potential actions in the here-and-now. Far more promising religious phenomena have faded even faster than such tabloid curiosities as weeping icons and the eyes of Mary discerned on a mildewed wall. Any careful reader of the New Testament, confronted with the *What Would Jesus Do?* challenge, would be well within the bounds of realism to ask "Which Jesus are you referring to—the itinerant rural teacher of the first century, the concealed Messiah revealed in his resurrection from the tomb or the divine second person of the Holy Trinity—and *when* must your Jesus make the choice you're proposing? Must he choose now or within some parallel situation in his own lifetime in Roman Palestine?" (The most difficult question of all lies further behind, as it lies behind all thinking about the life and meaning of Jesus—is it even remotely possible to imagine Jesus of Nazareth confronting twenty-first-century realities? Far easier, surely, to imagine Cicero in today's American Senate or Cleopatra at the helm of a major international fashion house. As with the Buddha or any other long-gone teacher, perhaps our only realistic hope is to ask "What would a given principle of such-and-such a teacher require us to do in a certain instance?")

The same careful reader of the Gospels mentioned above might also be justified in asking "What *wouldn't* Jesus do?" A whole sub-department of useful speculation could sprout from that direction. Presumably Jesus would have done many things after his resurrection that he wouldn't have attempted beforehand. Set down in Manhattan or the Rockies tonight, he'd surely respond in new and—as ever—unnerving ways. Above all, anyone who considers what Jesus might or might not do should first be firmly aware that he or she is *not* Jesus; and for many Christians, that's a hard mental feat.

As a useful caution from that direction, it's worth pondering (for instance) the classic Christian defense of warfare that founds itself on Jesus' disruption of the Temple moneychangers—Jesus exerted force against those polluting the Temple; therefore, so may (or *should*) we combat our own brand of enemy. There seems little question that Jesus exerted physical force in the episode, however physically damaging that force may have been to other men and women; but it's highly debatable that he'd have held his action up as a model of later behavior for any distant follower. A Jesus possessed of contemporary rhetoric might well say "I'm Jesus and you're not. If I choose to perform a ritual cleansing of the Temple of my people's cult, that is my choice to make, not yours—in whatever parallel situation you think you may have discovered."

In any case, the novel in which the WWJD movement had its origin was published by Charles Sheldon, an American Protestant minister, in 1896. That was a time when the so-called social gospel of Jesus was at the fore of liberal Christian thought and before scholarship had begun to raise its most insistent questions about the authenticity of various reported sayings of Jesus. After learning of the WWJD phenomenon, I recalled that, as a churchly boy in North Carolina in the 1940s, I'd heard of Sheldon's *In His Steps*; but it was only recently that I found the book still available, in several editions. Before I began reading it, I was fully prepared to condescend to what I suspected was a work of dated popular piety; but Sheldon's narrative, while it does move within the familiar frame of pious story, often countered my expectations. No student of the history of the novel is likely to set *In His Steps* high in the Western canon, but Sheldon's invented situation is interesting, and his prose is serviceable enough to have earned his many million readers through more than a century.

In brief, an unemployed and homeless young man—put out of work as a manual typesetter by the advent of linotype machines—arrives in a small American city. He attempts to find employment and encouragement and is everywhere rebuffed. At last he comes to Sunday service at a Protestant church. Toward the end of the hour, he stands and begins to tell the congregation of his astonishment at finding such blank rejection in a community that prides itself as Christian and thus implicitly welcoming, as Jesus was, to the poor and needy. No sooner has he expressed his bafflement than he collapses on the floor of the church, is rushed to a hospital and soon dies. The leaders of the church are belatedly chastened; and after careful discussion, some of them pledge to live for a year—to face all institutional and individual moral choice—under the guidance of the single question "What would Jesus do?" The remainder of the novel spells out the consequences, successful and less so, of their experiment.

Can Charles Sheldon's question—and its recurrence many decades later in the lives of a small group of Midwestern teenagers and then in many others—have any real use in the lives of mature persons of an ethical intent whose understandings of one Jewish teacher named Jesus are perhaps more complex, if

not more significant, than those of earnest adoles-
cents? And can the question have any meaning for
someone who's not a Christian or even for an enemy
of institutional Christianity? As the start of an answer,
I might wonder—again, with different names—how
useful it would be to speculate, at a moral crossroads,
"What would the Buddha do or Confucius or Lao
Tzu or Francis of Assisi or Dorothy Day or Flannery
O'Connor?"

As long ago as 1957, the English poet and critic
Stephen Spender told me that he often asked himself
at a crucial moment, "What would E. M. Forster do?"
Certainly the author of *Howards End* and *A Passage to
India* might well be an interesting figure to consult
(the best of his six novels probe as deeply as any into
the riddles of Western morality). Though an avowed
pagan, Forster was the stern yet brilliantly comic con-
science of a whole generation of liberal Englishmen;
and the moral quandaries faced by his Edwardian and
early-Georgian characters are as fresh as new paint
today, especially as we only begin to pay the agonizing
bills incurred by the death of European imperialism
and our own gross American debits.

Caught as I was by Spender's statement, I've often
asked a different question in subsequent years, especially when faced with business decisions in my writing career—"What would Charles Dickens do?" (In
the business department, I sometimes suspect that the
answer is "Dickens would do pretty much anything
you can imagine, this side chicanery" and that perhaps
I need another dead model—my deceased first literary
agent, the eminently incorruptible Diarmuid Russell,

or the somber Thomas Mann.) When stalled at a crossroads of decision in my private life, I have a very short list of past names whom I attempt to consult as un-self-servingly as possible—two of my teachers, the poet W. H. Auden and the biographer and critic Lord David Cecil, and my aunt Ida Drake, the nearest I've known to an actual saint. Surely almost everyone has some figure from the past, or conceivably the present, who might serve as a personal oracle—if consulted with as little self-anointment as possible.

5. THE CORE OF HIS ETHIC
AND WAYS TO EMPLOY IT

I'll put aside, for now, all questions of how many of the canonical words of Jesus were actually said by him or how accurately the Greek texts of the Gospels approximate his Aramaic words and on how many occasions he said a particular thing and then altered his wording or his emphasis later. And finally I'll dispense with the mountainous complexities of the ethos in which Jesus taught—the political situation of his time, the varieties of Judaism which he encountered and inhabited, the accidents of his own life. With the ground cleared momentarily then, it's interesting to assume that all the sayings are authentic and then to see if a usable and reasonably consistent ethic, sacred or secular, can be extracted from them.

At once we're faced with the contradictory sayings. In Mark 10.2–9 Jesus makes clear that all divorce is

wrong, that it literally produces adultery in its survivors; yet in Matthew 5.31–32 he allows a man—a
generic man, not an individual standing before him—
to divorce his wife in the case of her sexual infidelity
(nowhere does he discuss the possibility of a woman's
initiating divorce for whatever reason). Throughout the
Gospels, Jesus denounces wealth and the wealthy in
the most scalding terms—a repudiation that subsequent churches have generally suppressed or sped
past with an embarrassed glance toward the better-
dressed pews—yet he seems to have had wealthy
friends and supporters of his ministry whom he didn't
condemn (or perhaps condemned with a rueful smile,
reflecting the smile he'd extend as they're escorted to
Hell on Judgment Day in the Reign of God).

And in the always interesting matter of sexual
behavior, while Jesus deplores lechery, he's far less
concerned with sexual ethics than are his immediate
and present-day heirs in Christianity—a religion
almost uniquely given to agonies of sexual guilt,
intolerance and bouts of repression that have ranged
from the merely frigid to the murderous. At a minimum, Jesus appears to suggest the avoidance of fornication, adultery and any form of sexual harm to
children. In his two encounters with sexual wrongdoers, however, he displays the expected compassion—with the woman who "loved much" (Luke
7.36–50) and the woman caught in adultery (John
8.1–11), though he does laconically suggest that the
latter "sin no more." Any present-day reader is compelled to wonder whether Jesus never encountered a

male in sexual error; or is it a now-repugnant symp-
tom of his time and place, or of his own ethic, that
his only two such encounters are with women? Why
no men caught in rape, child molestation, incest, or
intercourse with menstruating women—among
other possible offenses? The Law forbade most such
relations; but male dominance likely prevented their
coming to Jesus' active attention, as it still shields
most male sexual wrongs.

It seems inescapable then to conclude that Jesus'
own views on many moral and ethical questions were
elastic enough, within bounds we can no longer establish, to respond to the natures and needs of particular
human actors embroiled in specific dilemmas which
were brought to his attention on given occasions. And
any attempt to simplify or codify his ethic, or to con-
dense it into a small set of sayings or even a single sentence, seems initially misleading or even wrong. Yet a
long-sustained curiosity has compelled me to make
such an attempt.

And any search for a single command that compresses the heart of Jesus' ethic must pause soon, wherever it ultimately settles, at Mark 12.28–34. There in the
Passover days immediately before Jesus' death, a lawyer
approached him in the Temple courts and asked him
"What commandment is first of all?" It had been a
week of ominous tension between Jesus and the
authorities; and Jesus must have sensed that, after his
messianic entry on ass back and his disruption of commerce earlier in the week, his own fate was sealed.
He'd now given all his enemies, of whatever persua-

sion, the evidence they needed of his real danger to their establishment and therefore their power as individual actors in a Temple state. But he answered the lawyer's question with a sovereign calm.

> "The foremost is, 'Hear, O Israel! the Lord our God is one Lord; and you shall love the Lord your God with all your heart, and with all your soul, and with all your mind, and with all your strength.' The second is this, 'You shall love your neighbor as yourself.' There is no other commandment greater than these."

Jesus is quoting, precisely, two commandments from Jewish scripture—the first from Deuteronomy 6.4–5, the second from Leviticus 19.18. The command to love one's neighbor as oneself had been much commented upon by earlier rabbis and has since been much studied by Jewish and Christian teachers who've speculated on the implications of the Hebrew word translated *neighbor*—who is one's neighbor? Is it only a member of one's own race, religion, tribe or family? Is it a member of some larger group, perhaps the entire human race?

Leviticus 19.34 specifies—most unexpectedly and movingly (after the devastations leveled by Joshua in the Hebrew conquest of Canaan)—that one's *neighbor* includes the stranger in one's midst:

> "'The stranger who resides with you shall be to you as the native among you, and you shall

love him as yourself, for you were aliens in the
land of Egypt; I am the Lord your God.'"

The elaborate codes of separation between Jew and
Gentile which had developed by Jesus' time, in Temple and synagogic Judaism, had apparently obscured
this scriptural command. The codes had likewise
diluted the ancient Middle Eastern tradition of a dig-
nified but open-armed hospitality—a tradition that's
strong still in many Muslim countries.

Many sects of Jews and liberal Christians, since
the nineteenth century at least, have generally chosen
to read the Levitical injunction in that broad sense—
my *neighbor* is any other human being with whom I
may come in contact or about whose need I learn. In
Mark's account of the lawyer's question, Jesus quotes
the injunction without defining *neighbor*. Luke 10.29
offers a significantly different, and far more resonant,
complication when the lawyer specifically forces the
question on Jesus—"And who is my neighbor?" Jesus
replies at once with one of his two most famous parables, the Good Samaritan. A Samaritan stranger,
despised by so many good Jews, is the only passerby
who tends to the "half-dead" man (whether the man
is a Jew or a Gentile, Jesus doesn't say). And the meaning of the parable, as Jesus proceeds to elicit from the
lawyer, is essentially this—a neighbor is one who
shows mercy to the needy (as the needy is the mercy-
giver's neighbor); and note closely that, as so often with
Jesus, the virtuous person is the *despised* person.

Anyone who today wishes to consider what Jesus

of Nazareth might have done in his lifetime, or suggest doing at any present crossroads of moral choice, could hardly do better than reflect upon a single command, Jesus' own reiteration of Leviticus 19.18: "'You shall love your neighbor as yourself.'" His yoking to that command the majestic *Shema* from Deuteronomy 6.4–5—"'Hear, Israel, the Lord our God is one Lord'"—provides an insistence that no human relation can proceed with any pretense of a moral foundation unless it moves within a monotheistic framework of love for one supreme god, a world that allows no one to escape from a single revealed ethic into the ethic of another god or goddess or some allegiance to an abstract but all-justifying deity like money or sexual craving or the sight of one's own precious face in a mirror, adoring what it sees.

My earlier acknowledgment that perhaps the ethic of Jesus—saying by saying, parable by parable and (what's so often forgot) deed by deed—is a virtual parallel to the ethics of earlier Jewish scripture may be technically correct. If we view the teaching and the actions in a body, though; and if we set them within the bare but credible narrative framework of Mark's Gospel, surely we're forced to glimpse an even more spacious moral vision in the process of formation, a process that's confirmed and completed by the mystery of the resurrection and Jesus' acts and words therein, whatever the resurrection was—or might be still if modern recording machines had been present and had been able to preserve some intimation of the reality of the phenomenon.

*   *   *

From the moment of his rising from the dead, the import of the stringent ethic of Jesus' prior lifetime becomes even more broadly imperative and more demanding on the moment-by-moment intelligence of every thoughtful person. That extensively enunciated teaching, however, is suddenly transformed and reduced, very quietly and in the simplest rhetoric of all, to the thrice-repeated command which the risen Jesus speaks to Peter in John 21. That encounter comprises a dawn appearance to seven disciples by the Sea of Galilee and is far the most imposing of all resurrection scenes, both in the implications of Jesus' few acts and words and in the power of John's plain but uniquely convincing narrative (Homer and the writers of a few scenes from Genesis and the lives of Saul and David in the First and Second Books of Samuel are John's only prior equals in the art of narrative; and Tolstoy is his only successor).

In the wake of Jesus' two Jerusalem appearances to them, seven of the disciples have returned to Galilee; and Peter has led them out onto the lake for a nocturnal fishing expedition. They catch nothing all night; then as dawn breaks, they see a mysterious figure on shore who directs them to cast the net one more time. When the catch proves large, "the disciple whom Jesus loved" recognizes that the man on shore is Jesus; and he tells Peter, who (in impulsive Petrine fashion) leaps into the presumably chill April water and swims for land. When the others have brought in the bursting net, and joined Jesus and Peter, the Lord feeds them—not the fish they've just caught—but fish and bread which he's somehow acquired and has prepared over an open fire.

When they've eaten, Jesus proceeds to ask Peter three times, "Do you love me?" As Peter's guilt-stricken perplexity forces from him three confirmations of love that rise in their intensity, Jesus merely tells him— merely!—"Feed my lambs," then "Guide my sheep," then "Feed my sheep." (The translation is my own. The Greek verb translated as *feed* can also mean *tend*. The Updated New American Standard says "Tend My lambs," "Shepherd My sheep" and "Tend My sheep." The difference perhaps lies in my choice of *feed*, which may have a less proprietary connotation than *tend*.)

One of the most interesting aspects of the scene is one which I've never heard discussed—what Jesus *doesn't* do in this appearance, the last recounted in the Gospels. Above all, he has extremely little to say or do. In the bare lines of the scene, once the full net is hauled ashore, Jesus' words seem addressed solely to Peter; and only the overheard tone of Jesus' voice, which John's prose makes no attempt to convey with adjectival or adverbial help, could have told us whether the words are conveyed as commands or requests. We are not even told whether the other six men in the scene overhear the exchange with Peter (verse 20 may imply that Jesus has led Peter away from the others). And the long, and for John, entirely crucial moment comes only in John's final resurrection account—a scene and a Gospel which many

modern scholars do not consider a reliable guide to the actual words or deeds of Jesus.*

My own long-considered feeling is that the passage reflects both a reliable command from a teacher who has now conquered death, and an irreducible compression into words, of the meaning of Jesus' entire life and work; and our uncertainty as to whether the words are whispered to Peter or spoken as resoundingly as the Sermon on the Mount is a further indication that the ethic of the *risen* Jesus is transformed, perhaps drastically so. I also think that the passage reports the outlines and some of the all-but-inexpressible details of an actual resurrection experience, an external and palpable experience that was not the mere result of a post-crucifixion evolution within the mind and heart of Peter. And it's worth our noting again that even the other disciples, who are surely nearby, are not necessarily included in the injunctions or the pleas to Peter. Is Peter being given a special duty, and does that duty confer upon him the primacy he seems to have

*I've discussed at length the origins and early history of the Fourth Gospel in my own *Three Gospels*. Briefly, it seems likely to be the last written of the four. Its author and date are still the subject of much uncertain discussion; but as early as the second century, it was dated in the reign of the Emperor Trajan (AD 98–117). And equally early, the patent differences between John's narrative and sayings and those of the other Gospels not only delayed its acceptance into the canon but also led to its being called a *spiritual* Gospel. Clement of Alexandria is reported to have written, late in the second century, that "John, last of all, aware that the bodily facts had been set out in the Gospels, was urged by his pupils and divinely impelled by the Spirit, composed a spiritual Gospel." I take that to be a way of saying that John was inspired to write an *interpretation* more than a literal history of Jesus' acts and his meaning.

acquired as the Jesus sect grew from these moments onward?

If we go a step further, however, and take the words as useful commands not only to Peter but to all human beings—and if we define *lambs* and *sheep,* as Jesus apparently did, in the same broad sense as *neighbors*—then an unequivocal requirement of love toward all creatures (certainly all human creatures) seems inescapable as the heart, the seed, of Jesus' ethic. Even in his earliest days, after all, he'd insisted in Matthew and Luke that the unconditional love of all creatures is an eminent characteristic of God, though he seemed to insist that God's love is tempered with judgment.

Implicit in any broad acceptance of the requirement to feed Jesus' sheep, however, is an understanding that Jesus, and no one else, remains the shepherd of the human flock—in each of the three injunctions to Peter, he describes the sheep or lambs as *his,* Jesus' own. In light of that implication, what he seems to require of Peter—and perhaps all other human beings—is a watchful and protective care for *all* those in need of care, though it would be possible to argue that Jesus' sheep are only those who believe in the Gospel of John's supreme fact—that Jesus is the Son of God the Father and is the only means of approach to the Father. Further, since sheep and lambs need guidance from their shepherd, sometimes a painful form of disciplinary guidance may be inescapable. And since a few sheep in almost any flock will ultimately be butchered to feed human beings, the injunction may also develop implications that are far from simple (as the often tyrannical, and even murderous, behavior of many Christian churches has shown and continues to show).

So an attempt to define the ethic of Jesus in the briefest possible form is by no means simplistic. Each of the supreme moral teachers is finally an aphorist since, by definition, ultimate wisdom is simple, though terrible in its difficulties. And shorn to that essential, the ethic of Jesus surely resides most adequately in a single compound sentence—*Feed my sheep; feed my lambs* (there's an important difference between an adult sheep and a lamb, in terms of the animal's need for nurture; and recent crises involving the abuse of children by clerics make this distinction crucial). As with the word *neighbor*, I'm compelled by Jesus' prior deeds to assume that his *sheep* comprise the entire human race, and perhaps numerous other live creatures.

With such an inescapable aphorism in mind, lately I've found myself considering three stubborn questions of a great and enduring moral force in many of the world's secular and religious communities. Despite their force, nonetheless—and the fact that they've hardly become more pressing today than they may have been in some parts of Jesus' own world—they're questions which he never encounters in the scenes of the four Gospels.

The dilemmas are homosexuality, suicide and the place of women in society and especially within organized worship; and however complicated a task it may be to wonder what Jesus would require, or request, a thoughtful human being to do when faced with any of the three dilemmas, I continue to wonder. The first two questions (of individual sexual fate or choice and of the decision to end one's life) have related closely to my own life since my early adult years; and while the second (the role of women) has not borne in upon me with heavy personal weight, it nonetheless arises from a reality that I've steadily encountered in a lifetime of loving female family and friends and from more than forty years of teaching young women and men in a first-class university.

Since I've made no extensive study of the historical development of Christian ethics, and am not a deeply read theologian, any offering I could bring to a discussion of such bristling questions would come most naturally—and, I hope, most usefully—from the discipline in which I've worked for nearly fifty years: the writing of imagined narrative. *Imagined narrative*, in this instance, is not a euphemism for *fiction*. I've written a good deal of fiction—stories, long and short—which I've entirely invented or have constructed with only the occasional use of small fragments of my own memory or the memories of friends.

I've also, however, written a quantity of narrative which attempts a sober degree of responsibility to the facts of my own life and the lives of family and friends (whose names I've actually employed) yet which awards itself the freedom to extrapolate connections, motives and results when real life has stinted me on such news. Perhaps my imaginative narratives are only another department of historical fiction, an often despised form. Yet I know historical fictions which have given me a far richer sense than I've found in scholarly biographies of the entirely possible reality of a few ancient lives. Thornton Wilder's *The Ides of March*, Marguerite Yourcenar's *Memoirs of Hadrian* and Mary Renault's *The Persian Boy* (the middle volume of her Alexander trilogy) are salient examples.

Brevity alone, if nothing more, bars me from making extensive claims for the Jesus stories offered below—brevity and, I hope, a sturdy awareness of personal limitation as well as a considerable knowledge of the existing drab warehouses of lifeless Jesus stories generated by all sorts, from pious clergymen to charlatans to lunatics to hateful enemies or even honest outsiders like Norman Mailer in his *Gospel According to the Son* (and behind all such attempts lies a whole library of ancient Jewish narrative speculation, called *Haggada* or *Midrash*, on the meanings of sacred story and teaching). Yet I'll also admit to having a plaque over my study door which preserves an encouraging remark of William Blake's, an artist who—of all people—knew whereof he spoke: "Imagination is evidence of the divine." What serious intender ever set out without some such hope behind him?

6. A FIRST SPECULATION: JESUS AND A HOMOSEXUAL MAN

The first dilemma constitutes a question which presently torments the American Christian churches and those of many other nations as well as some branches of Judaism. With the hardly surprising news that the Roman Catholic priesthood contains many active homosexuals, the question of sexual intimacy between persons of the same gender has evoked new and disturbing divisions—even hatreds—in almost all the wings of institutional Christianity. Even greater suffering is experienced by millions of homosexual men and women, in many nations, who are convinced of their own Christianity but can find slim welcome (or none) in perhaps a majority of American churches. And however inadequate the curiosity may seem, anyone interested in the mind of Jesus and in his ethic can hardly avoid wondering what Jesus might have done had he been confronted, as he never is in the Gospels, with an individual's homosexual behavior or—if an attempt were made to bring him forward in time—with a homosexual couple who intend a life together or even with those homosexual men and women who desire the blessing of the church or who long for ordination as priests and ministers.

Given the laws which are still on the books against homosexual intimacy in numerous American states, it's questionable how honest homosexual respondents are likely to be when questioned by pollsters; but careful surveys in the United States indicate that somewhere between 4 and 8 percent of American men and women admit either to having engaged in homosexual intimacy after the age of eighteen or they think of themselves as exclusively homosexual. Obviously such figures represent a substantial number of human beings in the rich hand of national minorities (for comparison's sake only, some 13 percent of Americans are of African origin; some 2.3 percent are Jewish); yet as such, homosexuals are the only substantial, and partially visible, minority who can be safely denounced in many of the oldest of mainline American churches.

Yet it's an extraordinary, and increasingly famous, fact that the early Jesus sect preserved no saying of their master's on the subject; nor did they invent one, though there are several indications in the later books of the New Testament that the early sect encountered the reality of sexual desire and performance between members of the same sex and that more than one elder felt compelled to confront the question of its acceptability.

The fact that no first-generation follower had preserved a saying of Jesus to guide the early sect in the matter may mean several things. Either Jesus was never confronted with the question, or he assumed that the condemnations contained in the Law were sufficient replies to the question, or he thought such behavior to be (for whatever reason) something which he could not condemn. In a passage from the Sermon on the Mount at which I've glanced earlier, he endorses the old Law resoundingly.

> "Do not think that I came to abolish the Law or the Prophets. I did not come to abolish but to fulfill. For truly I say to you, until heaven and earth pass away, not the smallest letter or stroke shall pass from the Law until all is accomplished. Whoever then annuls one of the least of these commandments, and teaches others to do the same, shall be called least in the kingdom of heaven; but whoever keeps and teaches them, he shall be called great in the kingdom of heaven."
>
> Matthew 5.17–19

What that affirmation means for contemporary Christians of whatever stripe — especially in light of the fact that, in the immediately succeeding verses of Matthew, Jesus himself annuls more than one of the Law's commandments — is a matter considered later here.

It's hardly possible to maintain that Jesus himself, a man who traveled in the company of vigorous young men likely deprived of regular sexual access to women, would never have encountered homosexual behavior or the moral questions which arise from it. Anyone who's lingered today in cultures where young men are strictly segregated, by social or religious custom, from close contact with women may well have observed a readiness on the part of many such men to satisfy one another's sexual needs in ways that range from the hygienic matter-of-fact to the adolescent-sentimental and the firmly committed.

And we have copious evidence that homosexuality was both prevalent and tolerated throughout the Roman empire and its ongoing predecessor, the even more far-flung empire of Alexander the Great (Alexander was, not at all incidentally, an unquestioned model hero who was famous for his love of his longtime companion, the male Hephaestion). Jesus, as a native of "Galilee of the Gentiles," would have known, or at least observed, a wide range of ethnic types and customs; and sex between pairs of men and between women would almost surely have been a familiar matter if not a necessarily more visible one than in similarly small American towns today. Yet when Paul, some twenty-five years after the death of Jesus issues his own apparent denunciations of homosexual behavior, he doesn't claim to have prior authorization from his master. And the New Testament letters written in the name of Jesus' brother James and of Jesus' own disciple Peter likewise offer no mention of the subject, much less any counsel, though the First Letter of Peter claims to be written from Rome itself.

No one needs to delve extensively into contemporary Christian debates on the matter to find that they're far more characterized by heat than by any usable light. And all the denunciations rest finally on condemnations found in the Old and New Testaments— condemnations which are ceaselessly repeated with little acknowledgment of the social orders out of which they arose or the behaviors actually described by the Hebrew or Greek words of the original texts. The proof texts themselves reside in Leviticus 18.22 and 20.13 (which seem to denounce male/male anal intercourse, the first text calling for exile "from among their people" and the second for the death penalty), in Paul's Letter to the Romans 1.26–27, in his First Letter to the Corinthians 6.9, and in the First Letter to Timothy 1.10 (again this text is almost surely not by Paul, though it claims to be). In the two latter texts, there is legitimate question as to which forms of behavior are referred to by the Greek words.*

But there's no serious question that both the

---

*Sane discussions of these important textual questions, and a good deal else, may be found in John Boswell, *Christianity, Social Tolerance, and Homosexuality* (Chicago); Tom Horner, *Jonathan Loved David* (Westminster); and Robin Scroggs, *The New Testament and Homosexuality* (Fortress).

Hebrew Law and Paul of Tarsus condemn certain forms of intimate relations between men, though (again) it's no longer possible to say which of the numerous forms of intimacy were abominable to those who drafted the proof texts. And Paul's is the single voice which has proved more potent than the voice of Jesus in forming the sexual Law of the Christian church and in thereby condemning the lives of countless men and women over two millennia. Interestingly, the Hebrew Law does not explicitly condemn sexual relations between women, though Paul may do so in Romans 1.26 (there the offense is so vaguely described as perhaps even to indicate female acceptance of anal penetration by males).

One glaring inconsistency has been frequently pointed out in the ongoing debates on the subject. If Jews and Christians are to obey these particular demands and avoid every form of genital intimacy between men (and perhaps women, in the case of Christians), then why are Christians not likewise compelled to obey all other scriptural commands—both Christian and Jewish—including those commands in Jewish law which control dress (no mixed fibers in clothing), diet (no pork and shellfish, no mixture of meat and milk, among numerous other taboos), no intercourse with menstruating women, elaborate purification rites for men who experience wet dreams, and Jesus' ban (or severe limitation) on divorce, Paul's uncompromising ban on significant roles for women in church affairs, his requirement that women's heads be covered in church, and so on, more or less endlessly?

Christians who labor to pick their way through scriptural Law and decide which commands they— and their neighbors—must obey and which they may ignore wrap themselves of course in miles of hopelessly tangled string; and the resulting daisy-picking spectacle ("Ah, I like this one but not that one") would be an occasion of high comedy if its implications had not proved so tragic in so many lives, ancient and modern. Any clear-eyed reader in search of a single of Jesus' appalling sayings, from several for instance, which the churches have heartily throttled in their recent exaltation of family and "family values" should focus for as long as possible on Luke 14.26—words which he delivers to "large crowds," not to some inner group of ascetics.

> "If anyone comes to Me, and does not hate his own father and mother and wife and children and brothers and sisters, yes, and even his own life, he cannot be My disciple."

Oddly, what I haven't encountered in the contemporary Christian talk and writing on the subject of homosexuality is a quantity of sustained concern with the possible response of Jesus to the question. One of the most distinguished New Testament scholars of the recent past—Raymond Brown, a Catholic priest—faced the implicit problem in one of the final products of a prolific career, his *An Introduction to the New Testament*; and he answered it with unaccustomed rashness—"Jesus himself, walking among us in our times, would not be frightened by being considered sexually and politically 'incorrect.'"*

In other words—or so I read Brown—in a world where liberals promulgate their code of "political correctness," Jesus would not have hesitated to denounce sexual intimacy within genders. To be sure, Jesus did not fear to travel against the grain of first-century Jewish Palestine; yet despite my speculations above about first-century sexual behavior in Galilee and Judea, we have virtually no evidence of the day-to-day sexual mores among Jesus' particular friends, followers and enemies. No large group of people known to me has been especially rigid in observing the moral codes of its religion, and that laxity especially pervades the realities (often so furiously concealed) of sexual behavior. What Raymond Brown failed to acknowledge in this connection, however, was that we do have ample evidence of Jesus' calm patience, and apparent tolerance, in the presence of several forms of sexual behavior condemned in the Law—prostitution, adultery and heterosexual cohabitation outside marriage.

To be as precise as possible, the forms of sexual behavior which Jesus deplores or denounces by name, or by unmistakable implication, appear to be these:

—fornication (the Greek word *porneia* covers the general concept of sexual immorality). The same Greek word is used in Matthew and Luke when Jesus gives lists of wrongdoing.

—adultery and (far more stringently, in Matthew

*The statement comes on p. 530 of Brown's *Introduction*, at the close of an interesting section of his chapter on 1 Corinthians, "Paul's Critique of Fornicators and Homosexuals."

5.28) the mere looking at a woman with lust in one's heart, which Jesus makes equivalent to adulterous intercourse. In Matthew 19.16–22, when a rich young man asks Jesus what he must do to "obtain eternal life," Jesus tells him to "keep the commandments." When the man asks, in effect, "Which ones?" Jesus gives him an interesting list of six—the first forbids murder; the second, adultery. No other sexual acts are mentioned to the young man as forbidden.

—causing "these little ones who believe to stumble." In Mark 9.42, in light of Jesus' extraordinarily caring reference to children, *these little ones* is most likely a synonym for *children*, one of whom he's just embraced, not for *humble believers* as students often suggest; and given the severity of the punishment which Jesus imagines for such misguidance, the harm he deplores is likely to be the molestation of children. Though there seem to be no specific bans on sex with children, or excessive child punishment, elsewhere in the Bible, our growing awareness of the awful frequency of parental child abuse—including incest—may well lead us to wonder whether such crimes were not, at some points at least, in the minds of the drafters of the Law.

In the case of fornication, Jesus goes no further in defining or denouncing the act than to mention it in a list of sins that proceed from within the hearts of human beings. Beside that plain fact, we must lay the seemingly undeniable fact that he keeps company with women who are likely to be prostitutes, perhaps even with male prostitutes. In Matthew 9.11 the Pharisees asked why he dined with "tax collectors and sin-

ners." It has frequently been assumed that these sinners have wronged the sexual Law of Israel (certainly
the woman "who loved much," in Luke 7.47, is implicitly a sexual outcast). And Jesus is never recorded as
urging those particular sinners to reform.

In the matter of adultery in John 8.3–11, his rescue
from a potential stoning party of a woman apparently
caught in the act of adultery concludes quietly as her
accusers depart in shame after Jesus' clever rebuke. He
then goes no further than to tell the accused woman
nothing more emphatic, or verbose, than "Go and sin
no more." His advice implies her guilt. Whether Jesus
had heard credible evidence against her or whether
we're meant to assume he possessed supernatural
knowledge of her guilt, the text doesn't say. Not at all
incidentally, it's one of the most typical of New Testament stories about women in that it takes no real note
of the possible wrong done to this woman by at least
two absent men—her husband and her putative lover.

In the matter of unmarried cohabitation, I've
looked above at Jesus' pleasant (even teasing) conver-
sation at the well with a Samaritan woman—the
woman whom he knows to have five former husbands
and a present male partner who is "not your husband"
(is he someone else's?—in which case, the woman is
committing both fornication *and* adultery). Because of
the woman, Jesus spends two days in her town but is
never recorded as criticizing her private life.

Of sexual wrongs, then, only the crime of harming
children—in whatever form, sexual, physical or mental—elicits the grim and especially vivid condemnation from him in Mark 9.42 (the passage, glanced at

above, is worth full attention—the millstone speci-
fied in Jesus' warning is one large enough to be worked
only by a donkey).

> "Whoever causes one of these little ones who
> believe to stumble, it would be better for him
> if, with a heavy millstone hung around his
> neck, he had been cast into the sea."

And as members of the Roman Catholic Church
have lately learned of the sexual violation of minors by
many priests, bishops and archbishops—and the
Catholic clergy has, by no means, a corner on this
offense—they have at least a specific saying of Jesus to
guide them as they gauge the severity of the wrong
(given the Christian church's tendency to excessive
degrees of punishment, it may be worth noting that
Jesus makes no personal attempt to drown a child
molester nor does he instruct anyone else to do so). In
the absence of detailed guidance from the foundation
voice of Christianity—Jesus himself—in the matter of
sexual condemnation, how then can virtually the entire
Christian church, its ministers and many millions of its
adherents, almost always respond to what they themselves define as sexual sin with the rapid conviction and
fervent condemnation they so readily display?

With no claim of personal or institutional authority
then, I'll speculate on what Jesus might have done in
a face-to-face encounter with a homosexual person. I'll
speculate in the form that comes most naturally to
someone who has lived by storytelling for more than

forty years. I'll invent a scene, entirely imagined but set in the first century and suggested to me not only by the urgency of its moral dilemma but by a hint that has long intrigued me in Paul's First Letter to the Corinthians. I've mentioned that, in the fifteenth chapter of the letter, Paul gives us the oldest surviving list of the persons who saw Jesus after his resurrection. The first two items in the list are these—"He appeared to Cephas, then to the twelve" (*Cephas* is the English version of Peter's Aramaic nickname *Kepha*, the one conferred by Jesus, meaning *rock*). The fascination for me, in Paul's list, lies however in a reported appearance to the Twelve.

Matthew 27.3–5 says that the traitor Judas, once he'd learned of Jesus' condemnation by the Sanhedrin, returned his blood money to the priests and hanged himself. But Acts 1.16–18 says that Judas kept the money and bought himself a field where—at some indefinite point during the forty-odd days of the risen Jesus' presence among the disciples—he fell, burst open and died, requiring the election of a disciple to fill Judas' place among the Twelve. It seems almost inescapable that Paul's preservation of a traditional resurrection appearance to the Twelve means that the risen Jesus appeared, in whatever form, to Judas before that wretched man's death. Why not? If one were to imagine being the risen Jesus, wouldn't one seek out Judas very promptly? The earthly Jesus had shown a concern for the despised man or woman that virtually surpassed his interest in others. Once he's left the tomb, who—of all the living—is more despised than Judas? The only problem I can see in such an assumption is the question of how the encounter would have been narrated to anyone who wasn't present, but a serious narrative craftsman can imagine credible answers.*

In the following scene I imagine Jesus—in the not-initially-recognizable physical form described in all four Gospels—encountering Judas Iscariot, now tormented by despair. None of the Gospels gives us a clear sense of why Judas betrayed his master, though the Gospel of John several times mentions Judas' love of money; and numerous old and modern retellings of the story have invented motives ranging from Satanic possession to a desire on Judas' part to compel Jesus to trigger the miraculous arrival of the Reign of God. In my scene, I imagine a motive for Judas that I've never seen attributed to him elsewhere—he loved Jesus completely. As always, I'm unsure in claiming any *first* in connection with Jesus studies; but here, in any case, is an imagined meeting between the two men. I've made no attempt to reproduce the language and method of any older Gospel, though I've hoped to think at least one honest way into the mind of Jesus and possibly the baffled and bitter Judas, of whom we know nothing but the fact of his betrayal.

✟

Since Thursday night—after Jesus' arrest and the scuttling off of the other traitors, called loyal disciples—

---

*The inevitability of a resurrection appearance to Judas has interested me for a long while. Some thirty years ago, I wrote a poem, "Instruction," on the subject—my first attempt to imagine such a scene. I include it here, as an appendix, in the version which appeared in my *Collected Poems*.

Judas Iscariot has slept in a cave three quarters of an hour's walk south of the Temple. The cave is hardly bigger than a marriage bed, and only a dwarf could stand straight up under its ceiling. But tall as he is, Judas has only left the cave twice—both times in the dark—to scrounge a little bread from the huts in the gully. The dogs have put up a scary howl; but any cur that's come near enough to smell Judas now has tucked tail and run. He needs another day or two of silent lurking. Then he needs to sit up and think of the next step to take from here. He's had very few contented days in his short life—he's nineteen years old—but since Thursday night Judas estimates he's been at least as desolate as any human south of Galilee except Jesus' mother and maybe Mary from Migdal, though he knows both women will come out of this like dew-washed lilies.

It's Sunday dawn and even the south sky outside his cave has lifted enough to send light in to where Judas sleeps on his right side in sour clothes too thin for early spring in the high hill country. When the sun has stirred enough life in his feet to waken him, he purposely lies with both eyes shut and—for the first time—he prays to die. He's fingered the notion of suicide since well before he and Jesus and the ragtag sycophants walked down from Galilee a week ago. He was that low down before they left; but it was only when they reached the city, with the crowds who parceled Jesus out in hot handfuls, that his dream had finally folded inside him.

Wild as it was, it had never seemed crazy, his dream of Jesus—surely not wilder than a few of the dreams he'd seen come to real life in flea-bag towns like Cana and Capernaum: all that excellent wine from water, a dead girl raised, three blind men's crusty eyes coaxed open and any number of pickers and scratchers soothed and silenced. So once the desperation swamped him, Judas cashed in and sold the secret news on Jesus to the priests—that this one man claimed to be king of God's new kingdom that would crash in on them with burning angels any day—and now there's plainly been no way to go but a private death down here where the mongrels, hawks and glossy crows will leave very little to trouble the neighbors.

He's loved Jesus that much, and as he lies in the early light—his eyes still shut—Judas pictures Jesus' face as strong as he'd seen it by torchlight two nights ago in the terrible garden. Even then, no other face had owned Judas—owned him way past chains or slavery. Yet to point Jesus out to the waiting guards, he'd strode up and kissed him hard on the lips. Jesus had said "Nothing but this?" And before Judas managed a Yes or No, the guards had bound Jesus, hand and foot; and his last look had parched what was left of Judas. Nothing to do now but finish the job, and nobody left but himself to do it.

Judas feels down his left side—his sensible ten-inch knife is waiting. Even better maybe, his long rope belt is coiled near the knife. Hanging will be both cleaner and slower and will draw fewer flies. So that much is settled, and what else is there but a little more sleep? No one down here will recognize his corpse, but most of the ones he's seen in the huts appear to be Jews. They'll bury him at least, whatever's left. He opens his eyes. He's still on his right side; the cave wall should be the one thing he sees.

But a man is lying, propped on his left arm, in the narrow space between Judas and the wall. The light's dim this far inward, but Judas is sure this is nobody he's ever known or seen. His hand of course goes straight for his knife.

The man says *"Judas,"* though. And—worst of all—the voice is Jesus, no doubt on Earth.

In the next slow moments, there's a little more light—normal daylight, nothing weird—and Judas sees better. The face is more than a little strange, but the voice has Jesus' unmistakable pitch and grain. Judas' fear quits at once, and something worse pours in. *Maybe he's done what he said.*

The face is a good deal younger than Jesus' face, lately at least; and the coat is maybe new tan linen— no rips or stains. Then the man holds his right arm up; and the wrist has a deep drying wound, the size of a square Roman spike.

Judas is almost entirely calm and can't think why. He says "Sir, it's you?"

The man says "Me. Where am I, please? And what day is it?"

Judas says "It's Sunday morning and you're alone with a boy you once knew—Judas Iscariot—south of the Temple in a cave I hope is safe for now."

Jesus glances to the narrow door of the cave as if some long arm might lunge in, and he whispers "Are we still on the run?"

Then a cold wave of understanding breaks over Judas, and he knows the whole story or the plot anyhow. He tells Jesus slowly "Toward the end, you said you'd rise from the grave—remember? This morning."

Jesus takes a long pause, though his eyes never leave Judas' face. Then he all but smiles and says "I haven't seen you since the garden, yes?"

Judas says "Yes sir."

Jesus says "You brought the guards to the garden?"

Judas says "Yes sir."

Jesus waits again, then his smile slowly broadens. "You want to say why?"

Judas reaches and almost touches the man—or the sight he sees. Is it truly a man? His hand draws back. Better not to know, not yet. It may be his own assigned demon, here to claim him. Well, the only immediate question is *Why?* Assuming for now it's the dead man returned, though, Judas can freely donate the answer. He faces this pierced sight before him—this man far finer even than the light that now spreads hot on both their legs—and he says "I loved you, sir, completely."

Jesus says "And I loved you—loved you all. Otherwise, how could I have stood so much misunderstanding for so long?" Jesus' smile is intact.

But Judas can't let himself veer off. It crosses his mind that this new Jesus has truly smashed the second commandment—he's made himself a thoroughly adequate likeness of God, the face and eyes and powerful hands. So Judas says "Sir, listen to me now please, for a change. I loved you from the day I first saw you—loved you on sight, completely, sir."

Jesus says *"Completely?"* as if that were news. But then he says "I understood that."

Judas says "Pardon, sir—you understood *what*?"

"That you wanted all of me," Jesus says.

Judas says "I did, more and more by the week. And you let me stay?"

Jesus says "I thought that love was love so long as neither party was a child and that no one's mind or body was hurt."

Judas says "But the Law means to kill me."

Jesus nods. "I seem to recall it does."

Judas says "No doubt about that, sir. If Hell's really waiting, I'll fry in Hell."

Jesus says "You won't" and this new certainty lights his face in the best old way and a whole new one.

Judas says "How'll I escape it then?"

Jesus says "Because I'm now the proprietor of Hell—Hell and Earth and all the rest. I think I'm somehow assured of that now." He seems to be smiling, but he also means it.

Judas says "So I could have lived with you then, if we could have just got off from the others? It was awful to lie down night after night with all the others scrambling to be nearer."

Jesus says "No way you could have lived with me. Remember how seldom I touched anybody who hadn't asked for help? That was who I was—"

Judas says "Every flake of my skin begged for help every day I was with you."

Jesus says "More than one person wanted that help from me. That was likely a wound I never meant to cause. I couldn't heal that anyhow." He stops to think. "Maybe I never tried."

Judas says "I never asked to be healed, sir. I never

felt sick, just starved even worse than I'd been as a child."

Jesus waits through another space that seems as long as a week of sleep. Then he says "What would you have done with me if I could have been yours?"

Judas says "I'd have tried to find some place to love you."

Jesus reaches up to stroke the dark ceiling as if it were one more thing to heal; then his hand points to the opposite wall, a yard behind Judas. The two men are safely cupped in on three sides—safe for now. Jesus says "This cave is as far from the world as I've been, except for the grave. What could we do here, once we'd really touched?"

Judas says "I'd find ways to feed us anyhow. When things calm down behind us in the city, I could lead us east and find a place to live beyond the river. You could start a builder's business. Don't forget I'm the best stonemason you know—the best one not working on the Temple at least." He pointed back behind them toward the Temple. "We'd keep you a secret as long as it took."

Jesus says "And you'd never love anyone but me, completely, I mean—anyone else's skin?"

Judas says "No sir, not completely. You'd be all I needed."

"No rivals ever?" Jesus is still smiling a little but the question's serious. He means to know.

"No rival, never," Judas says. By now he's almost halfway back from his will to die, and the weight that's aged him in these past days begins to lift. He looks almost his age again.

Then slowly as if his joints are decades older than his face, Jesus sits upright. His left hand comes out, taps the bone of Judas' hip and rocks it slightly. He says "Please understand—I'm not fully back yet. I may be able to see you again before I'm gone, and we can talk clearer. But this may be what I have to say, the thing I know—you need me, yes; but you also need every man, woman, child, dog, bird, snake, rock, tree and fish every moment forever. I think the hard part is all that *love*. What can be left over for any one person or creature or thing? I think nobody's law but mine is going to count from here on out, and all my law requires is love. Didn't I say it to you and the other boys at our last supper? Isn't that all I ever really said—that you should love each other the way I'd mainly loved you?"

Judas says "Yes sir" but he shuts his eyes again, tastes the old bitter cud he's chewed for so long and thinks *What earthly good is that to me?*

Jesus seems to have heard him. He says "The hard part from here on out is, what can *love* mean?" Twice he opened and folded again the palm of his right hand. The flexion pulled on the wound in his wrist, but no more blood threatened to flow. Now he was fully understanding who he'd been, what had happened in the past three days, where he was and why he'd come here. In his mind he repeated the last four words he'd said to Judas, "What can *love* mean?" From where he was now, they seemed all he'd come for— all that anybody could use from the wreck of his work, his life, his body and the fresh life budding up in him now. So he tried the words one more time on Judas.

"All I'd ask for now is love for everything equally. Of course the pain will likely kill you."

Judas thinks *That'll take far longer to learn than I've got.*

When he opens his eyes, Jesus' eyes are still a little dazed, still coming awake. He says "Judas, it's me here with you now—" It may have been a question.

If so it's an easier question than the one about what *love* can mean. Even Jesus' usual smell is strong in the space between them—a smell like fresh sage. Judas' left hand comes up to touch Jesus' arm.

By then it's missing. Jesus—the man who'd been here anyhow—is gone.

Judas clambers toward the door of the cave. No sign of the same man anywhere. Judas breathes the dawn air, as nearly clean as any air that reaches this valley; and though it clears a spot in his mind the size of the palm of an average hand, he can't imagine for more than three seconds how to stand from the huddled crouch he's in and find a usable path ahead. He knows he's seen Jesus back alive. He thinks he's halfway heard of a way to move elsewhere and find a whole life. He also knows he's loved the only man—or rock or stream—he ever means to love.

Before another half hour has passed, Judas is hanging dead from a dead tree fifty yards south. At least he found a limb high enough to leave his bare feet just past the reach of all but the biggest neighbor dogs. He'd left his sandals wedged in an even higher notch, a small good deed for whoever might find them.

✠

I'd, no doubt, be among the last to know whether that story is of any use in the pained and angry debates which continue to obscure calm reason in the matter of homosexuality and faith. Again, I've attempted a credible moment—in the right time and place—in which Jesus contemplates an enduring mystery, the full implications of his injunction to "love one another, even as I have loved you" (John 13.34); and I offer the scene as a piece of work that arrived with no conscious planning. Once I'd settled on the idea of a post-resurrection meeting with Judas and Judas' revelation of a passion for Jesus, the story came quickly. That's not to say that it arrived in anything resembling an inspired trance-state or even as automatic writing; but a reader might be interested to know that it chose its present course with almost no conscious forethought on my part and that its narrative and the exalted simplicity of Jesus' speech to Judas seem to me, in retrospect, to be un-self-serving at the very least.

Perhaps I'm, after all, assuming some subliminal external guidance in the course of whatever argument may result from the scene, though I'd ask no one else to make that assumption. Still, coming from me, the fact that it offers no solution to the old dilemma of homosexual proclivity is a little surprising. What comes most unexpectedly for me in the words ascribed to Jesus is a set of assertions that—while they're entirely implicit in his canonical resurrection sayings—may at first sound more Buddhist or Hindu than Christian. But then Jesus was not a Christian.

7. A SECOND SPECULATION: JESUS AND A SUICIDE

The second ethical concern here is suicide. Despite two sustained episodes of disabling depression in my adult life, I've never yet felt any trace of a wish to kill myself. I take no credit for the fact, and I have profound sympathy for anyone who reaches the point where the continuance of life—or the hurt he or she presently feels by the *instant*—is unthinkable. Given my own good fortune, it may seem odd that suicide has been an act that I've thought and read a lot about, and both the act and its inevitably tragic effect on survivors have appeared several times in my stories, novels, poems and plays. As I began to think of Jesus' possible approach to human dilemmas which never confront him in the Gospels, I was more surprised than I should have been to realize that—in a life which I think of as generally calm—I've had contact (ranging from intimate attachment, through long acquaintance, to close contact with their survivors) with at least thirty-three men and women who attempted suicide, twenty-four of whom succeeded.

The first of those occurred in my early childhood and involved kinsmen or in-laws, so I heard family discussions of the subject from the time I can remember discussions. Since all the Christian denominations to which members of my family belonged were Protestant—Methodist, Baptist, Presbyterian and Episcopalian—those kinsmen were not denied Christian burial as they might have been if any of them had been

Catholic at the time. But I think I recall overhearing, in early childhood, family discussions of whether a man who killed himself was damned to Hell (no woman we knew had actually tried it till I was four or five). The fact that Jesus again had left no crucial word on the subject may well have been mentioned, yet I'm convinced that audible speculations about the damnation of suicides ceased when my mother's favorite sister made an earnest attempt to end an exceptionally long depression. In any case, it's worth considerable pause to consider that the early Jesus sect either didn't possess or, again, failed to invent specific guidance from their vanished Lord on a matter that was a common mode of honorable death among the Romans and that soon was a major concern of the persecuted band who refused to make a required ritual sacrifice to the emperor— were Christians who boldly courted martyrdom also courting suicide?

Hebrew and Christian scriptures are, perhaps oddly, ambivalent on the question of suicide. Some heroic figures from both traditions are either outright suicides or ones who at least seem willing. Obvious examples are Samson and King Saul, the three young men in the Book of Daniel who choose to enter the fiery furnace rather than renounce their faith; and Stephen, the follower of Jesus, who seems to choose death for what his accusers call "blasphemous words against Moses and against God" (Acts 6.11). In the third century Origen suggested that the Gospel of John asserts that Jesus himself chose to die (in John 8.22 some bystanders, hearing Jesus' apparent allusion to his forthcoming death, say "Surely He will not kill

Himself, will He?"). To be sure, in Mark 8.34 Jesus urges his followers to "take up [your] cross and follow Me"; and large numbers of his early followers took a similar course through the avenues of Roman martyrdom with sometimes eager enthusiasm.

In the fourth century, with woefully enduring power, Augustine denounced suicide as a form of murder, largely on the basis of the sixth commandment in Exodus 20.13, "You shall not commit murder." And thereafter the Catholic Church moved gradually toward a condemnation of the act which rose to a peak in the definition of suicide as a mortal sin and the denial of burial rites to suicides. The major figures of the Protestant Reformation did not relent in condemning self-killing; and as late as 1790 a generally quiet Anglican priest—the revolutionary John Wesley, the founder of Methodism—went to the alarming length of advocating the public exposure of the bodies of suicides as a deterrent of self-murder.

Modern findings in medicine, psychiatry and sociology have contributed to a more complex understanding of the act in its various manifestations and to a slow yielding in the view of some—but by no means all—Christians and Jews. Only as recently as 1983, for instance, the Catholic Church relented in its official denial of burial rites to the self-killed. And even now as the incidence of suicide has continued to rise in America, and as we've heard numerous discussions of the moral right of individuals to choose to end their lives in the face of terminal suffering, most of the mainline Protestant churches and Orthodox Judaism continue to view suicide as the forbidden taking of a life.

The result continues to be what it's been for centuries—though suicide as a salient dilemma doesn't disturb Christian communities nearly so audibly now as homosexuality or (in many churches still) the religious rights of women, few common realities cause more individual and familial pain than the church's now mostly silent condemnation of the act, and therefore the person who performs the act. As recently as a few weeks ago, when a friend of my family shot himself dead, I heard several otherwise feeling acquaintances remark upon his death as a matter of personal choice, even as an act of conscious vengeance on the living.

And the survivors of suicide—mates, children, parents, lovers, friends—are still left with perhaps the most desolate feelings possible in the wake of any adult death. As distant as I was from my family's recently self-killed friend, I've watched a close relative suffer intensely from that death; and I've therefore spent a good many moments trying to think my way into the mind of a gifted young human being who walked uphill on an early spring morning with a loaded gun and then paused to turn it against himself. His nearer relations have all their lives to think the same thoughts and with a far greater sense of loss. Only the survivors of a murdered child are likely to be left in sight of a more bottomless-seeming abyss, with so little hope of recourse.

Those who remain in the wake of a suicide, however, might find the beginnings of a justified ease in considering the possible response of Jesus to the choice of death or the irresistible compulsion to die in the face of unbearable further life. My second venture in the

imagined ethics of Jesus describes another meeting in
which the risen Jesus has sought out Judas Iscariot,
who as the Gospel of Mark says "handed him over" to
the religious and civil authorities and triggered his
death (this Judas is a very different sort of man from my
prior Judas; he's older now and far harder-bitten by
life). Also like the prior story, it came with little conscious forethought beyond a life's reading and reflection (in fact it surfaced as I wrote the above-mentioned
essay for *Time*). Judas has left Jerusalem in the turmoil
of Jesus' arrest, walked the four miles south to Bethlehem and has spent two nights there.

✢

Judas rose in deep silence. His childhood friend
Hamer, Hamer's two sons and his pregnant wife were
lying on the same dirt floor in the same room; but they
never so much as flickered awake when Judas tied on
his sandals once more and left for good. He'd learned
his destination yesterday as he and Hamer walked
round the village. Where Hamer had told him the
locals were claiming Jesus was born, there'd been a
dead tree—a bare black snag above the cave where,
even now, a few lamps had burned and a handful of
flowers drank water in a jug. Judas had gripped the
snag, even then, and chinned himself once. It was
still firmly anchored. Hamer seemed to get the idea
and smiled his narrow smile.

So now as the sun broke free of the hills and swept
the fringes of Bethlehem, Judas reached the tree again.
He'd cadged a stout piece of rope from Hamer's, and

he set straight to work. Throwing the rope up and over the strong limb, he started trying to recall the right knot. He mustn't fail at this too. But with all his years of learning scripture—and these last months on the road with Jesus—he'd lost the knotting skills of his childhood on his father's scratch farm (Judas was the only one of the Twelve from outside Galilee).

Maybe five minutes passed—he was sweating anyhow—and a man's voice spoke from close behind him. "Need any help?"

Judas lurched around, thinking the voice was too familiar. But the face was indescribably changed. Jesus' old fire and wit were gone. This man looked—not remotely childish but utterly new, just born at sunrise, this April Sunday. So Judas said "All the help I need—thanks anyhow—would be for you to *leave*."

The man almost seemed to leave for a moment; his image faded on Judas' eyes. Then he was back and stronger still. His face had the calm that Judas had spent a whole life hunting. The man nudged Judas lightly aside, then reached up and tied the appropriate knot.

Judas somehow watched the man's broad hands and still didn't notice.

But when the man finished, he raised both hands toward Judas and said "Jude, go to your father now; he'll need you for the planting. It's not too late. The others won't harm you; I'll warn them off." The man's upright hands were pierced with deep wounds, just below the palms.

Judas thought *Those ought to be hard to see*, and

he gave the sight maybe five seconds to move him. But no, nothing came—his mind had clenched down to the size of a pebble in his skull. Still he looked through the two yards that lay between him and the man, and he studied the new face for any further sign that this was Jesus, keeping his promise.

The strange head began to nod, signing Yes; and slowly a kind of mist around the eyes began clearing. Finally the voice said "I've come to you first."

Judas never thought of fleeing. The one choice left apparently was to beg his teacher's pardon and then use the rope. So he asked the final question of all. "You're Jesus, aren't you?"

The head nodded Yes, though the eyes and mouth were entirely calm.

Judas said "If you pardon me, help me leave then." He reached up and seized the rope in both hands. He'd need to climb the tree to make it work.

The man took a long ten seconds to think. He even looked at the sky.

Judas suddenly thought *What's he know about farming? He's trying to figure if there's really still time for me to help my father with the planting,* and he almost wished for the guts to laugh.

But then the man looked back to Judas and said "Sure, I'll lift you." He did that silently with no strain at all, and he waited in place in reach of Judas' arms till the last breath failed, but Judas never once made another sound and never reached toward him.

✛

The fact that I've mentioned a recent encounter with suicide near the midst of my family may leave that second story open, again, to the charge of self-service—a Jesus who not only condones suicide but lends a hand in the act. My present reply would be, first, to insist that I in no way mean to condone suicide as a generally useful solution to any human problem, at any age.

Some seven years ago I sat by while a much-loved friend, dying of AIDS, worked his own silent way through the thought of killing himself. At last he chose to live, through terrible days and nights— finally helpless—till the virus finished with him. But he never asked my opinion on the prospect of suicide; and though I knew he could easily find the necessary fatal drugs, I never felt the right to say a word (what would I have done if he'd asked me to bring him the small handful of pills?). His family, some of whom were Catholic, were also at hand. Maybe his choice to endure was meant as a merciful gesture to us all—the name he'd chosen for himself, years earlier, was Lightning after all. In any case, the sight of his quietly astounding bravery in the grip of so many months of pain and bodily humiliation remains an ideal to more than one of us.

While suicide is among the last of human choices I'd encourage, then, I'd hope for as much human comprehension and mercy as any of us could muster if confronted with the threat or the reality of self-destruction. Second, I'd point out that the Jesus involved in my story of Judas' suicide is, again, the resurrected man, not the wandering teacher; and when

Judas cannot accept the suggestion of returning to his father's farm, Jesus does what may be the next best thing—he helps Judas die. Nowhere in the Gospels does he insist that life must be endured at all costs. And later here I'll attempt to explain what I see as the crucial difference between the choices and urgings made by Jesus in his first life and those he makes in his resurrection—those differences can almost entirely transform any discussion of Jesus' ethics.

8. A THIRD SPECULATION:
JESUS AND A DESOLATE WOMAN

Finally—though Jesus is accompanied on his travels through Galilee, Perea and Judea by more than a few women—he has only two recorded encounters in which he is alone with a woman. In John 4 (the delicious meeting by Jacob's well with a Samaritan woman), he begins by bantering wittily with the five-times-married and now licentious woman; and in John 8.11 (the aftermath of his rescue of the adulterous woman threatened with stoning), his few words to her are perhaps those she would most want to hear. Indeed, the sunlit and laughing intensity of the well scene and the sudden stillness of the rescue scene are marked by a calm clarity of focus which is usually found only in first-rate plays when the dramatist's sympathy is deeply aroused. Yet neither of those encounters involves a discussion that throws obvious light forward on the recent and still hotly controversial hope of women to play more central roles in various branches of Christian worship.*

The Gospels never say whether Jesus was married, nor is any woman portrayed as being in an especially close and enduring relation with him. All we know is that after Jesus' death, Paul remarks in 1 Corinthians 9.5 that Peter is married; but again he offers no information about Jesus and marriage. Indeed, in 1 Corinthians 7.25, Paul says that he has no "command" from Jesus on the subject of marriage and virginity. With few exceptions then, it's been assumed that Jesus—in what is, again, thought to have been a relatively short life—never married, despite the fact that rabbis mostly did so.

Whether any scandal attached to his being accompanied on his travels by women, we're not told (though the report in Luke 8.3 that Jesus was accompanied by "many" women who were helping to support him "from their own private means"—their personal earnings or some private inheritance unshared with a husband?—offers ample opportunities for the scurrilous or even the merely accurate observer). The presence of women among Jesus' road companions may have been unusual for the time and place. But while his enemies are on record as accusing him of numerous offenses, from demonic alliance to "eating with sinners" to permitting his disciples to eat food with dirty

---

*In John 20, Jesus may be alone with Mary Magdalene after she's discovered the empty tomb; but her use of the plural pronoun *we* in 20.2—"we do not know where they have laid him"—may indicate the silent presence of others, presumably other women.

hands, he's never quite accused—in the Gospels—of whoremongering or even illicit sexuality of any sort.

It's unclear how often other rabbis, especially itinerant teachers, gathered such a mixed band; and it's unknown what positions Jesus' female followers may have held among his disciples. Were they limited to the "woman's work" of food gathering and cooking and clothes washing? If any of them were wives of the Twelve, did they bring along children and older dependents? If all the wandering followers—male and female—were unmarried, or unaccompanied by spouses, can they have traveled all day and lain down at night with no trace of sexual desire or tension among them? It would require a far more blinkered view than I can muster of any sizable human group, of whatever sanctity, to believe that Jesus' companions were spared any such feelings, needs and hungers. And dim echoes of such actual difficulties may be audible in the Christian apocrypha of the second and third centuries.*

---

*An introduction to some of these echoes is provided in Pagels's *Gnostic Gospels*. In her third chapter, "God the Female/God the Male," she made famous a little-known passage from *The Gospel of Philip*, perhaps a third-century text, discovered in Egypt in 1945.

> ... the companion of the [Savior is] Mary Magdalene. [But Christ loved] her more than [all] the disciples and used to kiss her [often] on her [mouth]. The rest of [the disciples were offended by it . . .]. They said to him, "Why do you love her more than all of us?" The Savior answered and said to them, "Why do I not love you as [I love] her?"

The brackets stand for missing or partially legible words in the original manuscript or words that have been conjectured from the context by a modern team of scholars.

While the great majority of these frequently hare-brained late documents are of no use as witnesses to acts and thoughts of the historical Jesus, the *Gospel of Thomas*—a sayings collection which was discovered, in a full Coptic text, in Egypt in 1945—may preserve a few genuine sayings that are absent from the canonical four. The last of Jesus' sayings in *Thomas* is this response to an unexpected, yet not incredible, request from Peter.

> Simon Peter said to them, "Let Mary leave us, for women are not worthy of life."
> Jesus said, "I myself shall lead her in order to make her male, so that she too may become a living spirit resembling you males. For every woman who makes herself male will enter the kingdom of heaven."*

In any case, if a genuine saying lies—at whatever remove—behind these words, it's now impossible to know what Jesus may have meant.

Certainly nothing he says to or about women in the canonical Gospels resembles the saying from Thomas or suggests the need for any such radical change in female life. With the exception of Jesus' refusal to meet with his mother and brothers in Mark 3.31–35, his initial harshness in his meeting with the Syro-

*A full text of *Thomas*, translated by Thomas O. Lambdin, may be found—among the other documents of the rich Egyptian find of 1945—in James M. Robinson, General Editor, *The Nag Hammadi Library* (HarperCollins, Third, Completely Revised Edition, 1988).

Phoenician woman in Mark 7.25–30 and the chilly treatment which he accords his mother in the Gospel of John, Jesus generally appears to honor women, though he could hardly be said to deal with them warmly (his penultimate word from the cross in John attends to his mother's future care, though there again he addresses her only as "Woman"; and oddly she's never referred to as Mary in the entire Fourth Gospel). In general Jesus exhibits, to all but his outright enemies, if not an unqualified welcome then a patient forbearance that's hardly reminiscent of his prophetic forebears.

Even as he approaches Jerusalem for his final anguished visit, words burst from him which seem to reveal a layer of feminine tenderness that's rare in males at any time.

> "Jerusalem, Jerusalem, who kills the prophets and stones those who are sent to her! How often I wanted to gather your children together, the way a hen gathers her chicks under her wings, and you were unwilling. Behold, your house is being left to you desolate!"
>
> Matthew 23.37–38

Yet nothing he's recorded as doing or saying in the four Gospels suggests that he envisioned, in the coming Reign, roles for women which would have been remarkably different from those they play in the world of everyday first-century Galilee and Judea.

An attempt, then, to imagine a credible encounter

between Jesus and a woman who might challenge the limitations of those roles, or ask him hard questions about the life of women, is especially difficult. If homosexuals may hope to find room for themselves in the very silence of Jesus, anyone in search of his historical sympathy for the plight of women would seem to be up against a greater challenge. When I began thinking of an imaginary encounter which would explore such a relation, however brief, I felt at once that it would be easy enough to imagine yet another meeting between the risen Jesus and, say, Mary Magdalene—who, in John 20.11–17, sees him first—or with his mother or with Mary the sister of Lazarus, who did not hesitate to remark Jesus' failure to appear at her brother's sickbed before his death. We know from Mark 6.3 that he had sisters of his own, but they exist only in that verse, otherwise in deepest shadow. An even less familiar figure may offer greater promise, someone who stands at the center of a famous story but says only two words (in the Greek original and in English: "Nobody, Lord")—the woman who's discovered in the very act of adultery and whom Jesus saves from stoning.

In most contemporary editions of the New Testament, it will be found in John 8.3–11. But to abbreviate a complicated question, it seems undeniable (on the evidence of the oldest surviving texts) that the story was not an original part of John nor of the other canonical Gospels, though Jerome included it in his fourth-century Latin Vulgate translation, which became the canonical text of the Catholic Church and thus entered almost all later translations of the Gospel.

Raymond Brown says, in his edition of John, "a good case can be argued that the story had its origins in the East and is truly ancient. . . . There is nothing in the story itself or its language that would forbid us to think of it as an early story concerning Jesus." And he adds, interestingly, that the story may have been accepted late because "The ease with which Jesus forgave the adulteress was hard to reconcile with the stern penitential discipline in vogue in the early Church. It was only when a more liberal penitential practice was firmly established that this story received wide acceptance."*

Before I proceed to a third imagined encounter, I'll summarize the old episode as I understand it. Jesus has seated himself in the Temple courts and is about to teach a group which has gathered about him. But the lawyers and the Pharisees bring before him a woman whom they say has been caught in adultery. They remind Jesus that the Law of Moses requires that such women be stoned—stoning for adultery was still employed at the time (and in Nigeria recently two women were sentenced to death by stoning for adultery and sex without wedlock)—but they ask Jesus for his opinion in the matter. It's seldom noted, incidentally, that the text does not state that her death is imminent at the hands of these men, though paintings and films of the episode mostly imply that it is. What the story does specify is that they're testing Jesus, hoping to find some reason to accuse him.

The moment suggests that, by now, Jesus' enemies

*Raymond Brown, *The Gospel According to John*, I, p. 335 (Doubleday).

suspect him of excessive mercy in the treatment of sinners. But Jesus bends down and begins to write on the
ground in silence. What he writes, we're not told (the
Greek word can also mean *mark* and doesn't require
that Jesus was writing actual words). The woman continues to stand, in humiliation if not fear, in the midst
of the men. At last Jesus speaks — and I translate literally — "The sinless one of you first, on her, let him cast
a stone." As he speaks even that brief a sentence, it's
possible to see his finger pointing, in dramatic order —
now here, now there, to the relevant actors in the
scene and then to the cast-off builder's stone that must
have lain round the Temple courts, which were still
under construction. Those who hear Jesus depart,
beginning with the oldest (because they're wiser and
know when they're defeated, or merely because the
young men are deferential?). Jesus is left alone with the
woman. Standing, Jesus says "Woman, where are they?
Did no one condemn you?" When she says "No one,
Lord," Jesus says "I do not condemn you either. Go.
From now on sin no more."

And the episode ends with no further indication of
Jesus' next step or the woman's. I'd assume most readers take it that the woman departs at once and never
meets Jesus again. Considering how deftly the editor
finds a seam in John's original text, then neatly lays the
episode in, it's noteworthy that the editor makes no
mention of any disciples, or other followers, being
nearby. Yet how many readers consider where the
woman may be bound as she leaves Jesus? Can she
even think of returning to her husband? Surely they
have children? Where is her lover? If both men have

abandoned her, is any life other than prostitution imaginable for her now? Could she return to her parents for instance? In the long trail of Christian narrative speculation, it's likely that there have been attempts to imagine some further encounter between the two memorable figures; but I've run across no such stories and none are famous.

In my own exploration, as in my two prior stories, the invented action and talk arrived with no detailed planning beyond a desire to be both interesting and true to my convictions about Jesus' deepest nature, in both his earthly and his risen lives. I've given the woman a name which may have shaped her sense of herself from early on—Rahab, the name of the whore who gave Hebrew spies secret entrance into Jericho as they made their first approach to the Promised Land. While Rahab is specifically called a whore—or harlot—in Joshua 2.1, and is furthermore a Gentile, she wins rescue for her family when Jericho is sacked and the populace slaughtered; and she's listed in Matthew 1.5 as a direct ancestor of both King David and Jesus. If we assume that the woman's father named her (would a mother choose the name?), then we're at once free to wonder at his intentions for her life. Often, names become destinies. Here's my third story.

✚

When all the men left and Jesus told her to "sin no more," Rahab stood on still where they'd left her; and her eyes stayed shut. Anyone who watched might have thought she was waiting for the first stone to strike.

But Jesus was the only one watching from nearby, and he thought she might be picturing the man who'd run and left her alone when her husband opened the door on a sight so awful that he turned her over to a pack of men as shameless as she. Jesus wasn't sure that she'd been abandoned, but the Pharisees and lawyers hadn't brought the man along, and they likely hadn't killed him, so chances were that this woman was completely alone in the world. She'd given no sign of hearing what he told her—"Go. Don't sin again"—so he repeated it quietly.

And at last she looked up and met his eyes frankly. "Sir, why is it wrong?" Her left eye was bruised, and a handful of hair had been torn away above her left ear—blood streaked down her neck but was almost dry.

Jesus saw the point of her question though. What caught him most was how she put it—her forceful *why?* Who could doubt that adultery was wrong? Wasn't that half the point of committing it? Why else fling yourself on the risks? For a start he said "It's been wrong since long before Moses called it wrong—"

With a hand flat out before her in the air, the woman stopped him; and her voice was low but firm. "How wrong is it that my husband beats me far more times than he kicks his dogs?—and even the pitiful dogs aren't mine."

Jesus had no answer ready.

So the woman said "My name is Rahab. My father named me that; and it can still sting, knowing who she was."

Jesus said "I'm kin to the old Rahab—or so my father claimed (we're descended from David)." That helped him feel right in moving closer to where the woman stood. A few early strangers were trying to gather again to hear him teach. His eyes ignored them but his hands waved them off. He was at the south end of Solomon's Porch on a limestone bench.

Rahab came and sat beside him dubiously, a little more than an arm's reach away. The thought of a touch was unbearable now, but this man seemed unlikely to touch her. He'd quietly waited for her to speak, so she said "The man I was with when that mob caught me—he's never so much as raised his voice in all the time I've known him."

Jesus said "How long is that?"

She almost smiled as she looked slowly round them. "*Was*," she said. "You notice he's gone."

Jesus nodded and stifled the echo of her half-smile. It was worth recalling that murderous-hearted men had brought him Rahab only minutes ago. But at last he said "Where are the children?"

She said "*My* children?" as if he might mean the children of the Earth (none were visible here in the Temple courts, not this early in the day). "I've had five children. The first three were girls and have come along fine. Then my first boy was born cold-dead, no sign of a reason. The beautiful second boy suffocated before he was two—some heavy demon lodged in his chest till at last he just quit trying to breathe. He was in my arms when he finally went still and was gone for good. At the funeral my husband yelled across the boy's cold body that I was killing all his boys. He's never come near my bed again. The three girls, as I said, are growing; but my husband's mother took over from me when the last boy died, and I hardly see them ten minutes a day. I cook for myself, wash my own clothes, I tend a patch of garden and give whatever grows to the neighbors. My husband makes his own arrangements, with his mother and whoever else he needs or wants to see. He won't divorce me—for 'his own reasons,' as he admits, he won't divorce me." She spread both palms upright on her knees and studied them a long time. Then she scrubbed them both hard together and said to Jesus "Tell me—what's my wrong? What do I do next? You told me to Go. Where do I go?"

He waited even longer than Rahab. Then he said "You could join the women who travel with me."

"My husband would have me killed by midnight—his men are ready as you plainly saw. I doubt I'll live past dark anyhow."

Jesus said "We could hide you—we've hid a few others."

Rahab said "But they're saying you're not long for this world yourself."

Jesus said "I'm hated by a good many people, yes."

"So you want to die?"

Jesus said "You've talked to some of my students?"

She said "The man my husband found me with—you may not know him but he knows you. He's heard you talk a lot here lately—at night." She pointed east. "Down there in the valley, that cave where you sleep with the ones you trust. He says you're saying you truly want to die." When Jesus was silent for the longest time yet, she asked him again—"You want to die?"

Jesus' face showed the kind of shock you see on

boys caught out in a wrong they honestly didn't know they intended. He'd never heard any such question from another human being, much less a woman; and he'd never answered it, even to himself. But now he said "I may. Yes, I may."

And Rahab's curiosity was at least as deeply founded. "Then where does that leave these pitiful people who're following you? None of them look a lot smarter than me. None of them, surely, can take over this healing job you've started."

He tried to give her the truth she deserved, that he thought she'd earned in the past few minutes. It was a truth he could hardly bear. "They'll likely die, a fair number of them—the few that have loved me. Most of the boys can go back home and fish or cobble or plow their fields, but God help the women. Where can they go next? No man'll touch them now." As strong as he was, in face and eyes and arms and legs, he suddenly felt like a hopeless bet—unless he took this woman and ran. He paused a full half minute to think his way through that. Then he said to Rahab "Get up now and leave me at least."

"You still haven't said how I can live the life you've told me to go on living."

Jesus nodded one last time. "I haven't, no. Pray for me though please. God will very likely hear you."

She'd still not stood. "Why me, sir?"

"—Far more than me. God's calling me in, as a ransom for all the wrong ever done."

"You're saying He means to sacrifice you? Then why should I ever obey Him again, I or anyone else if He's truly that cruel?"

Jesus said "What other choice do you have? He'll love you entirely, whatever you do."

Rahab finally stood. She could see Jesus plainly meant every word; and to her stunned mind, it felt flat certain that what she saw as the torment of his huge misunderstanding was killing him at least as fast as all her life had already killed her. For longer than she'd ever have guessed, he seemed like the son that might have lasted her. She almost reached to stroke his hair, but his eyes were still caught in a worse confusion than any she faced—that God loved them both. She could see he believed it, and she felt that at last she'd learned to turn from men with troubles greater than her own. When she left him, she could feel his eyes on her back till she reached the great steps that led her down out of the present brief safety of the Temple walls and into the world of men and stones, crosses and nails.

✠

If it does nothing more, such a scene may remind male readers of a complex skill possessed by a great many women—they see and comprehend, far more quickly and deeply than men, the likely outcome of choices made by the powerful men in their vicinity (I wouldn't say that nearly so many men bring a similar skill to their observation of women). In this scene, Rahab combines her gratitude to Jesus for a temporary rescue with the rumors she's heard of his recent commitment to a sacrificial death—a death which, to her, must seem the equivalent of suicide—and she then concludes that this is one more man who can offer her no safe harbor from the dangers of life in a society like her own and ours.

Hers is much like the knowledge possessed by many other sentient creatures who exist far down in the hierarchies of their worlds and thus have no choice but to live from moment to moment in the possibility of deadly harm to both their minds and bodies. Any religion which fails to demand that its powerful adherents pay steady attention to mitigating the lives of those in such plights can hardly call its God a loving God—and virtually all men are far more powerful than they know.

9. AN OUTLAW CHRISTIAN

Such speculations as my own, however brief, run the risk that Albert Schweitzer described so relentlessly in 1906 in his *Quest of the Historical Jesus.* Among the several achievements which make that book one of the few revolutionary scholarly studies of modern times is Schweitzer's demonstration of what might have seemed an obvious conclusion—that all attempts to write lives of Jesus are doomed to discover the Jesus whom the author wants and needs to find. To be sure, that's also the probable destination of the writer who hopes to capture a full-length portrait of any complicated man or woman—Emily Dickinson or Einstein or even a child genius on the order of Mozart or Rimbaud. As Schweitzer says, near his conclusion, "The world affirms itself automatically."

Still, efforts to strain back against mere self-gratification can surely be made by any careful biographer. Schweitzer himself did so and, nearly a century later, the outlines of his boldest assertion are widely, if by no means universally, accepted by scholars—that while Jesus of Nazareth indeed thought of himself as God's ordained Messiah, he nonetheless died in the deluded belief that the Reign of God was imminent, a Reign in which Jesus believed that he would return in glory as the foretold Son of Man and in which belief he flung himself on painful death to ignite the coming down of God's rule. And in self-defense of my own patent fictions, I can at least point out that the risen Jesus offers Judas no endorsement of Judas' yearning for a passionate bond between them; that the risen Jesus' readiness to help the desolate Judas hang himself is quicker than I might have hoped for; and his dialogue with the woman caught in adultery lances an abscess of solitary dread in the earthly Jesus that I hadn't foreseen his revealing to anyone before his last night.

Yet to any reader who suggests that the Jesus in my imagined scenes shows none of those fierce aspects of his nature which are unquestionably on display at numerous points in the Gospel record, I'd concede the suggestion. Certainly the enemies of Jesus' work, whom Matthew and Luke tend (perhaps misleadingly) to identify as the Pharisees and whom John (far more misleadingly and disastrously) calls the Jews, come in for frightening condemnation from him. Even the Sermon on the Mount, with all its promise of the unstinting love of God the Father and its injunctions to refuse a violent response to violence, ends at

Matthew 7.21–23 with a bafflingly horrific prophecy of
eventual punishment on Jesus' own enemies.

> "Not everyone who says to Me, 'Lord, Lord,'
> will enter the kingdom of heaven, but he who
> does the will of My Father who is in heaven
> will enter. Many will say to Me on that day,
> 'Lord, Lord, did we not prophesy in Your
> name, and in Your name cast out demons,
> and in Your name perform many miracles?'
> And then I will declare to them, 'I never knew
> you; depart from Me, you who practice law-
> lessness.'"

I've mentioned, more than once, the problem of
apparent contradictions in the teachings of Jesus. I can,
however, find no unresolved contradiction in his
actions toward other human beings. And no clash in his
thought is harsher than that between these two
things—the consistency of Jesus' ethic of love among
human beings, an ethic which is the clearest mirror of
his most original faith (in the unfailing love of a fatherly
God for each of his creatures, a love which irradiates
and inevitably supplants the Law) and those sayings in
which he predicts the sufferings, and the eternal
damnation, that await certain evildoers. I see no orthodox way, in all the centuries of attempts of which I'm
aware, to bridge the contradiction.

Yet casting aside every Christian theology which
I know, and entering for a moment the realm of
unbound speculation, it's possible to imagine that
God the Father made an act of choice to kill and then

glorify Jesus by resurrection simply to disprove his Son's unstable misunderstanding of the completeness of God's love. Jesus taught the existence of a Father who was loving and unceasingly solicitous but also terrifyingly punitive. Millennia of Christians, and those who long to be Christians, have been—and are—repelled by the prospect of a God with two such unpredictable and unmatchable faces.

Surely, however, by his redemptive act in the killing and raising of Jesus, God proved the totality of divine love. Admittedly, the problem flowing from that assertion is one which Jesus himself never fully addressed—if our Father God is all-loving and all-powerful, where then does evil come from? Where else but, again, from God, though God might well say *I'll be the definer of the word* evil. *Who are you to tell me that, say, the rape and murder of a child is evil? I survey all of history, you survey a few decades, how can you know the meaning and outcome of anything?*

In any case, one who argues that Jesus means what he says about the love of God *but* who then adds that the love which Jesus promises—and the ultimate salvation—is conditional upon our obeying the Law of Moses is confronted with Jesus' undeniable assertion in Matthew 21.31 that "the tax collectors and prostitutes will get into the kingdom of God before you [the chief priests and elders]": that is, ahead of the more respectable members of his own society and I daresay many of ours. Those contradictions lie before any thoughtful follower of Jesus as a daunting succession of gulfs. Another difficulty for any serious student or would-be follower is that modern scholarship has left it impossible to judge with certainty when, early or late in his life, a given saying of Jesus might have been uttered (the single exception may be Mark 15.34, Jesus' dying words).

Since the terrible gulfs exist, if we had a reliable sense of the chronology of his convictions and demands, then we might weigh the polar components of his teaching more reliably and make our own decisions. Is there, in his thought, a visible process of growth or change like that in virtually all other thinkers? Is the man an eloquent but gravely confused, even psychotic, guide? Or has his teaching been hopelessly misrepresented by his earliest followers? — no other document in the New Testament denies the punitive aspects of the Father. Or are we simply free to say Yes to any one of these three possibilities and ultimately find ourselves in Hell for the error? Certainly a vast chorus of Christians would say that a Yes to the notion of a confused Jesus will land one in Hell very fast.

Any reader who's come this far is owed, by now, some profession of my own beliefs in the matter. In earlier essays and books, I've made it clear that I'm what in all honesty I can only call an outlaw Christian. Since childhood—for unrecoverable reasons having to do with the family history and surroundings of my early life, with early experiences that induced an irrational but defensible and durable faith, and with succeeding decades of experience and study—I've believed that Jesus of Nazareth stood in a uniquely near relation to the Creator of this universe and all the life in it. I can't define the nature of that relation, and

I couldn't attempt to weigh the degree to which the man Jesus participated in the godhead; yet I've never thought that he was simply a human being with extra-ordinary endowments of moral insight, fluency and healing power. My conviction of his absolute unique-ness is grounded, like Paul's, on two broad feet—a per-sonal visionary experience of healing from a dire illness and an early certainty that—in some entirely decisive, inexplicable but likely palpable way—Jesus rose from the dead.*

And to this day, I have no difficulty in reciting the traditional creeds of Christianity, the Apostles' and the Nicene creeds, though certain phrases remain obscure for me. The claim that Jesus was "born of the Virgin Mary" or that "I believe in the resurrection of the body," for instance, are matters to which I can give assent with as little comprehension as I have of other matters to which I nod with equal ease—say, the emerging (and apparently comic!) laws of particle physics: God has a brilliant sense of humor, as we might have guessed.

After a childhood spent in the churches to which various members of my family went, however, I came in early manhood to see that my own relation to God and his Son would best be pursued outside all churches. A mysticism that first appeared in my childhood, and was perhaps innate, was the strongest component in that decision. I'm most definitely not

*Since I've written about these experiences at length in three prior books, I won't expand upon them here. Anyone who's interested can find the discussions in my *Clear Pictures*, *A Whole New Life*, and *Letter to a Man in the Fire* (all Scribner).

referring to *mysticism* in the New Age sense of one who's vaguely *spiritual*. I'm invoking the older familiar sense of the words *mystic* and *mysticism*—dating from the seventeenth and eighteenth centuries—to describe one whose relation with God feels direct, not channeled through an institution or another individual.

Any such feeling has quite rightly been recognized by the orthodox churches as suspect, even dangerous—prone to atrocious pride or trivial absurdity or to contact with forces other than God. I was born during the Great Depression, and was largely reared, in a county with a black population of some 65 percent; so another large factor in my separation from church was a growing awareness, in the 1940s and fifties, that all white American churches (wherever located) were astoundingly indifferent to racial injustice. It's accurate, I think, to say that I heard no single word condemning or seriously questioning American, not to mention Southern, racism from the pulpit of my family churches or that of Duke University in my childhood and youth. Nor do I think that any prior member of my family, in the major Protestant churches of North Carolina, can have heard any such word from at least the end of the Civil War till, say, the mid-1960s (and the cliché continues to hold—no hours in America are more segregated than those of Sunday morning).

As I was awakening to the willful racial self-blinding of white Christianity, I also became aware of another blindness that was—if anything—even more inexplicable (racists did at least have, as a desperate warrant for their convictions, those passages of the

New Testament that urge the subservience of slaves to their masters). Then in the South, and widely elsewhere, many churches effectively ignored the plight of the poor, as they go on doing today—as I still do, socketed as I am in my deluxe surroundings and tended by warmhearted and reliable family and friends. Then, more slowly, I grew aware that the churches' intolerance of any forms of sexuality beyond the traditional choices of marriage or chastity left me a literal outlaw. The men I'd love, who'd love me in return—we could only meet beyond the barring doors of churches.

When asked my religious affiliation, I used to attempt to describe myself with the slightly less alarming adjective *renegade*; but the Oxford English Dictionary told me that a *renegade* is "an apostate from any form of religious faith, *esp.* a Christian who becomes a Muslim." Since I've never (by any means) been an apostate, *outlaw* was the next available choice and an accurate one. I live outside the law of almost any church; and I cannot think my principles immoral, though of course I make huge numbers of errors—from small to large—in my daily life. A few churchly friends have tried to persuade me that my presence in a congregation would be the practical way for me to join in efforts toward reforming at least some aspects of Christianity which are plainly in bald defiance of Jesus' life and work. Finally, I've been unable to agree. In loyalty to my mother's memory, and to my gratitude for its role in my youth and for its charities, I've retained membership in a particular church; but I haven't been there since her funeral.

There can be little doubt that, in two thousand

years, various wings of the church have done large amounts of good. So far as I can see, the major shares of that good have come in the lives of men and women inspired by Jesus' compassion to subsequent lives of sacrifice and service. Then a few of those servants have given to Western civilization its central master-pieces of literature, painting, sculpture, music and architecture. Remove Christian art from postclassical Western art and very little, prior to the 1880s, survives. Further, I have no doubt that—without some institution to keep the example of Jesus alive in the eyes of many, however distorted that example has so often been—his memory and his teaching would have dras-tically dimmed, especially in those centuries of wide-spread illiteracy and the ecclesiastical discouragement of any unmediated access to the Gospels.

Yet my own needs and my hopes of service have never resettled actively in a church; and it seems unlikely they'll do so now. A Lutheran friend and I share the sacrament of communion, and I of course attend the marriages of friends and the baptisms of their children. I make those confessions with no sense of pride or defiance, only (again) by way of honest self-description. The sense of religious community which many find in communal worship, however, has come to me—and come richly—through concentric circles of loves and friendships, through my teaching and reading, my writing and reflection.

10. THE LAW OF GRACE: GRACE ALL WAYS

Delivered of those confessions then, I'll move toward a conclusion by saying that the thing my three imaginary scenes may demonstrate more clearly than anything else is a certainty that has only grown as I've lived in steady relation with the figure of Jesus since childhood. While I know that I can't resolve, even to my own satisfaction, all the contradictions in his verbal teaching, I'm long since convinced by his recorded actions—all of which are informed by a compassion that relents only for brief bursts of anger at his enemies—that by the end of his life Jesus had become almost entirely antinomian, *against the Law*: the Law of Moses and the laws which humankind has made. We'll almost surely never recover the truth of Jesus' final beliefs about the nearness of God's Reign, his own role in that kingdom and in the lives which anyone else may lead therein (if anyone gets there). In all his resurrection appearances, he says no single word of entirely *new* ethical injunction.

In Mark 16.16—again, a passage not written by the author of the Gospel itself but added by a later writer when the actual ending of Mark was perhaps thought to be too abrupt, lacking (as it did) a resurrection appearance—the anonymous author speaks for the risen Jesus.

"He who has believed and has been baptized shall be saved; but he who has disbelieved shall be condemned."

In the Great Commission which is the last of Matthew's two very lean resurrection stories, Jesus requires the disciples to teach those whom they baptize "all that I commanded you"; but he doesn't reiterate any portion of that teaching or highlight its core commands. In Luke 24.47 Jesus reminds the disciples that it has been foretold that repentance for forgiveness of sin shall be preached in his name; and again, in John 21 he revises his entire ethical hope and compresses it into three words (four in the Greek), "Feed my sheep."

The Apostles' Creed asserts that, after his death, Jesus "descended into Hell"—a clause now omitted by some Protestant churches—and that assertion has more than one scriptural grounding, chiefly the claim of 1 Peter 3.18 that

> He went [after his death] and made proclamation to the spirits in prison, who once were disobedient, when the patience of God kept waiting in the days of Noah.

If we're to assume that the claim represents an effort by the early Jesus sect to explore the mystery of the thirty-odd hours of Jesus' death and entombment (and there are scattered hints throughout the New Testament of some such journey during Jesus' death), then we may even now fairly speculate that the risen Jesus knew more than he'd previously known of such matters as the soul's destination and its condition in the afterlife. And he saw no cause to warn those who met him, risen and glorified, of flames and agonies.

Whatever he learned in the hours of darkness, the ethical bareness of Jesus' resurrection sayings seems to me to establish beyond doubt that he'd at last come to see that the only Law with binding force upon us is the Law of Grace. And *grace* is the enlightenment, the strength and—often more revealingly, though terribly—the trials which God sends us in the hope that we'll more adequately rise to the work of loving our neighbors, ourselves, the remainder of creation and Himself.

In the mid-1870s the young Vincent Van Gogh labored miserably as a Christian evangelist in the coal mines and potato fields of southern Belgium. Slowly, though, the heat of his enthusiasm and his sense of mission turned his understanding of self and work toward painting. But his awareness of the force of Jesus remained strong in him through the richly productive but widely rejected and mentally troubled final two decades of his life. And only two years before his suicide, he wrote to his friend Emile Bernard—

Christ alone—of all the philosophers, Magi, etc.—has affirmed, as a principal certainty, eternal life, the infinity of time, the nothingness of death, the necessity and the raison d'être of serenity and devotion. He lived serenely, *as a greater artist than all other artists*, despising marble and clay as well as color, working in living flesh. That is to say, this matchless artist, hardly to be conceived of by the obtuse instrument of our modern, nervous, stupefied brains, made neither statues nor pictures nor books; he loudly proclaimed that he made . . . *living men*, immortals.

This is serious, especially because it is the truth.*

I'd as soon take the word of Vincent Van Gogh, even while his mind began its descent, as the word of any other witness or student of Jesus' life and work—Jesus made the human race immortal. For me, not only do the deep soundings of Van Gogh's art surface with a further validation of Jesus' claims—the painter's compulsion to see and transmit the abundance, benignity and terror of creation and even (unblinkingly) the mysterious torment of his last years is as cogent an argument as any theological contention, likely more so. And his description of Jesus rings an almost exact harmony to the understanding that grew, from the age of nine onward, in my own mind—the sense that the risen Jesus was, in all the world's landscape, the figure to watch and hear. That sense grew for me, as it apparently did for Van Gogh, the son of a Dutch minister, in the teeth of dozens of hellfire sermons.

Jesus of Nazareth was, above all, what he insisted he was in the last words of which we have any record—a watchful shepherd. We are meant to do no less than he asked with each live man and woman and child in our reach—to tend them as Jesus tended the souls he met in the hamlets and towns and cities of Palestine,

**The Complete Letters of Vincent Van Gogh*, III, p. 496 (Graphic Society of New York, 1959).

with patient healing and close attention to their all but endless needs (not *our* sense of their needs).

Once Paul experienced a shattering encounter with the risen Jesus, he spent the remaining three decades of an arduous life in declaring his faith in God's saving action through the death and resurrection of Jesus. In his authentic letters, Paul—a once devout Pharisee, as I mentioned—works strenuously to comprehend the meaning of Jesus Messiah for the eternal lives of individual Jews and Gentiles and for their ongoing daily lives in what he believed was the nearing shadow of the breaking in of God's Reign.* In that uncertain waiting-time, how much of the Law of Moses remained in force for them and for himself? And if the Hebrew Law was forever supplanted, as Paul came so near believing—and as he declared on more than one occasion (above all, in his Letter to the Galatians and most forthrightly in 3.24–25)—how should Christians behave? Quite literally, how should they respond to such important questions as the circumcision of male infants, marriage and the behavior of husbands and wives, the fulfillment of sexual desire,

---

*There is still no firm agreement as to which of the thirteen New Testament letters attributed to Paul were actually, or entirely, written or dictated by him. At present, at least seven seem unquestionably authentic—Romans, 1 and 2 Corinthians, Galatians, 1 Thessalonians, Philippians and Philemon. To some students, 2 Thessalonians seems uncharacteristic of Paul's theology; and both Colossians and Ephesians seem stylistically too graceful or elaborate to come directly from the often headlong Paul. 1 and 2 Timothy and Titus are even more noticeably different from Paul's usual style, and their teaching appears to come from a later stage in early Christian history.

dietary customs, the duties of slaves and masters, respect for civil authority and for anyone claiming spiritual authority over their individual consciences?

In Galatians 5.6, Paul says one thing that, while Jesus never said it (so far as we know), constitutes another summation of the entire essence of the risen Jesus' teaching and, supremely, the meaning of his earthly and his risen acts.

> For in Christ Jesus neither circumcision nor uncircumcision means anything, but faith working through love.

To attempt a minimal expansion of Paul's statement of Jesus' meaning, I'd suggest the following. *For anyone who believes that God has raised Jesus from the dead to be our line of access to the Father, through emulation of his compassionate mercy and through prayer, any call for an unexamined adherence to the old Law is no longer effective.* What is urgent now, Paul says, is only that same trust in God's grace as it works through love in our lives and in all our dealings with the world.

It's easy enough for many citizens of contemporary Western civilization, and great portions of the East, to glance at Paul's packed sentence—it's one sentence in the Greek—and to walk away, shrugging. Who, except Orthodox Jews and certain Fundamentalist Christians, now regards the Law of Moses with any degree of strictness? A partial answer is that all of us in the West, except malign psychopaths and willful villains, make most of our serious choices with the internal navigational aid of Hebrew Law—the Ten Commandments and a few other broad-gauged injunctions from Leviticus and Deuteronomy, with added shadings from the prophets. However frequently we choose to ignore that guidance, it's nonetheless the base of our moral and civil law; and no broadly acceptable replacement has been found except for the ethic of Jesus—*God loves us; we must love one another.* The moment-by-moment lifelong details of how to do so are our first, last and hardest task. And the two principles of Hebrew Law which Jesus saw as central may well prove to be anyone's best starting point, an irreducible foundation—we honor our neighbor so far as we may, short of violating our duties to God and to our own steady enactment of a just and measured honor for ourselves. (We cannot hope to honor a neighbor usefully if we cannot honor ourselves to an appropriate degree. "Love your neighbor as you love yourself" is a reversible command—"Love yourself as you love your neighbor" is an entirely necessary, and widely neglected, primary requirement.)

It's an endlessly hazardous ethic. Within its scope every human being stands as his own pope and priest, her own judge and jury. Aside from the police and the courts, the main guide resides in the words and acts of Jesus. As troubling as the daring of such an ethic still is—and as frightening as it is to consider what a good many human beings, presently curbed by the constraints of the traditional Judeo-Christian Law, might do if freed to their own devices—it's worth recalling that we've each been on our own from the very start of our species (whether we think it evolved with immense slowness on the plains of Africa or instantly in the molding hands of God as he made the first man and then, slightly later, the first woman from a rib of the man's).

Not for nothing did the Romans, expert in this matter as in so much else, agree with the observation of their playwright Plautus that *Homo homini lupus* — Man is the wolf of men. No one above the age of, say, five who is not chained to a wall and in the entire control of another human being has finally proved to be morally controllable at every juncture. And at how many crucial junctures are we not drawn by our inheritance as a predatory species and by our rearing as potential victims, in need of power for self-defense, to lash out and seize and tear?

To take the grimmest view of our natures, yet a view which is braced almost daily by world news and sometimes by the news of our small neighborhoods, we may turn to a dreadful but merely accurate statement by Rebecca West in *Black Lamb and Grey Falcon*, her famous account of the Balkans, that trustworthy theater of hatred.

> Only part of us is sane: only part of us loves pleasure and the longer day of happiness, wants to live to our nineties and die in peace, in a house that we built, that shall shelter those who come after us. The other half of us is nearly mad. It prefers the disagreeable to the agreeable, loves pain and its darker night despair, and wants to die in a catastrophe

that will set back life to its beginnings and leave nothing of our house save its black-ened foundations.

Founded though the ethic of Jesus is upon a faith in the hard-to-trust (because unseen and often silent for long stretches) love of a fatherly God, it foresees just such an enduring depravity in humankind. And no century subsequent to the life of Jesus has seen an abatement of our wolfish tendencies, though we do now know that the families of wild wolves are better organized than many of our own and perhaps more benign. Why else would Jesus have gambled so much of his moral capital on the command in Matthew 5.38–39?

> "You have heard that it was said, 'An eye for an eye, and a tooth for a tooth.' But I say to you, do not resist an evil person; but whoever slaps you on your right cheek, turn the other to him also."

You must not resist an evil person. A first consideration of the sentence might point out that, however early in his career Jesus may have pronounced the princi-ple, it certainly shaped the form of his own suffering and death. Anyone familiar with the topography of Jerusalem, and the nearness of the Temple to the adja-cent small Mount of Olives, knows that—had Jesus wished to escape the designs of the Sanhedrin on the night of his arrest—he could easily have slipped out of the Garden of Gethsemane in deep darkness, climbed the Mount and been on his way into the trackless Judean wilderness in a matter of, say, twenty minutes.

No command from Jesus has been, and is, more entirely ignored by Christians than Matthew 5.39; and no command is harder to contemplate accepting as a principle of one's own life, not to mention the lives of nations. Yet a reader as wise in the traits of humanity as Leo Tolstoy identified those words as the center of Jesus' beliefs. My own sense of the progression of thought that produced the command is this—we must not resist an evil person because, when evil comes, it descends upon us as the mysterious will of a God whom we must believe, in the long run, to be loving. And the long run can be very long indeed.

To take a single example, the history of Jesus' own people through at least the past 2,500 years is an ongoing testimony to that; but nothing in all those years—least of all the present tragic two-headed reality on the modern ground of old Roman Palestine—has assailed Jesus' assumption that resistance to force is doomed only to generate a cycle of vengeance as vicious and ultimately futile as the primal violent act of Cain or the hard demand of Abraham's Sarah that Ishmael should be exiled from his brother Isaac. W. H. Auden reduced the matter to four lines of his poem "September 1, 1939."

> I and the public know
> What all schoolchildren learn,
> Those to whom evil is done
> Do evil in return.

At the start I asserted that no other life and no other body of teaching have been studied, debated and warred over as extensively as those of Jesus. In closing I'd suggest that this sketch of that life, and this conclusion from its recorded sayings and acts, indicates that a reader might consider the following possibility. What God left to attentive creatures, when the risen Jesus vanished at the end of forty days, was an enormous but remarkably trim inheritance—the three sayings examined above (*Love your neighbor as yourself, Feed my sheep, Do not resist an evil person:* the command to *Love God* is implicit in each of those three).

Though each of the injunctions can be paralleled in earlier Hebrew teaching, their joined force in the mouth of a single man is trebled by the man's conquest of death; and perhaps even more movingly, by his brief life's patient acts of healing, forgiveness and teaching, all recorded in the barest minimum of words and gestures in four brief Gospels. Trim as the legacy is then—and perhaps no other enduring teacher can be contained in such a slender parcel—it requires tireless attention from anyone claiming to be its serious student.

My own attention has been lengthy, if hardly tireless or notably effective. And lately as I've shown, it's taken the old but, for me, new form explored in the three brief stories and one of the two appended poems. Whatever their failings, I repeat that any value I attach to their findings derives from my effort to lean as far backward as I can in the hope of avoiding a foregone confirmation of my own opinions (each story, in fact, comes nearer to contradicting my prior feelings than I'd ever have expected). I likewise am glad—and entirely for my own purposes—of the spontaneity with which they arrived, admittedly from a lifetime's reading and reflection.

That quickness gives them whatever freshness they offer; and while they make no effort at mock gospel-simplicity, the ease of their coming has resulted in a smoothness of texture that may encourage more free reflection on the reader's part than verbal density might have done. Still I'm far from insisting that they contribute significantly to moral or ethical discussion, least of all to anyone's moral debate. Should they ever do so, in a benign fashion, I'd be glad to know it; but they're, first of all, personal to me. As prior published attempts of my own have demonstrated, they're likely to outrage a number of readers; but so will almost anything written or said about Jesus—many self-labeled Christians outclass the spitting cobra in the quantity and range of their hurled venom.*

---

*Handy samples can be found in *Time*, the issue of 27 December 1999—a sprinkling of negative reader responses to my earlier essay on Jesus, with its apocryphal scenes. Since those scenes were remarkably respectful of Jesus' seriousness in all aspects of his life, it's interesting to wonder what could have pressed such poison from readers who presumably called themselves Christian. Was it simply that a great many Christians will not tolerate, under any conditions, narratives—in prose, film, onstage or otherwise— which imagine Jesus as a man who walked a particular patch of ground, in a certain time, and led a recognizably human existence, however distinctive? Somewhere I've read the estimate of one student, who'd carefully listed the actual events from Jesus' life described in the Gospels and calculated that every action reported therein could have been crowded into a three-week

Should I continue with narrative explorations, I'd
hope to work toward greater length and (eventually
perhaps) toward entering the minds of various forms
of Jesus—his unspoken thoughts, his visions, his dis-
coveries and defeats. That latter aim is a venture in
which no writers known to me have succeeded for
more than a few sentences at a stretch. The canonical
evangelists and even the later apocryphal writers avoid
the attempt to enter his mind, though they very occasionally describe an externally visible emotion in Jesus
(Mark 14.33, as I've noted, says that before his arrest in
Gethsemane "he began to be very distressed and troubled"; then it stops short of further exploring the
silence of that hour). But other ancient writers in the
West, with the exception of the soliloquies in Greek
tragedy, also give slim attention to the possibility of a
silent mental life for their heroes.

Whatever the cause of the awe expressed by the
Gospel writers at the fact that Jesus, after all, possessed

---

span (the physical acts, that is; John, of course, requires that Jesus
acted in Jerusalem on three consecutive Passovers). What, then,
would Jesus have done with the remainder of his time on Earth?
Luke, famously, implies that he lived for thirty-odd years.

I recall a popular radio show from my childhood, called
something like "The Light of the World." Each Sunday after-
noon some Gospel episode was dramatized; and whenever Jesus
was about to speak, there'd be a pregnant pause; then a few bars
of patently ecclesiastical music would sound, then Jesus would
speak (very likely in the King James translation) and further
music would echo his conclusion. As a child, I found nothing
strange in such proceedings—no stranger than the haloes emit-
ted by his head in pictures ranging from Leonardo to Sunday-
school pamphlets. Yet I also always knew that, if I saw him, he'd
bend and fold me into his arms—an even more welcoming man
than my father, himself the kindest soul I'd known.

a mind inside his skull (or wherever they thought the mind resided), we might well sympathize with their silence—given the image of Jesus that arose in Christian art from early on. If that traditional face in any way derives from the actual appearance of Jesus, who could have borne the gaze of those honest eyes for more than a day? To see only the most ancient of icons—the early-sixth-century portrait of Jesus still preserved in the monastery of St. Catherine in the Sinai desert—or the face on the Shroud of Turin (recent evidence suggests that the carbon-dating results of the 1980s may have seriously underestimated the age of the cloth and its image) is to be further astonished at the possibility that a man whose face radiated such power could have been the simultaneous source of so much mercy.

What would Jesus do—or think, before and after an act or a speech—at any number of imaginable moments that continue to plague the curiosities and actions of millions of human beings? More precisely, and more usefully for many, what would Jesus have *done* with any such dilemmas in his own time and place; and of what use might such speculations be for us now? Narrative leaps, prepared by serious reading, at comprehending both the mind of Jesus and the world that surrounded him might instruct any one of us, whatever our station or the range of our beliefs, doubts or outright rejections. The prime conveyors of his meaning to posterity—Matthew, Mark, Luke and John—are above all storytellers.

Though Paul, and perhaps a few other New Testament authors, wrote down their arguments and exhortations earlier than the evangelists, surely the memory of Jesus would have survived only as a footnote in the history of Mediterranean religions if the Gospel stories had not been recorded, as *stories*, and kept intact for our attention (a man went here and did that; then he went there and did another thing). Valuable as the quantity of sayings preserved in Matthew, Luke and John continues to be, it's Mark—with his utter faith in *story* and the narrative faith he taught to others—who lit the hearts of the later Jesus sect and spread its initially quiet flame beyond the eastern Roman empire and onward, for good and evil, into the world.

The curiosity then which lies behind my brief stories may constitute, at the very least, a serious way of wondering—a way commendable to anyone, of whatever persuasion, since most anyone is a seasoned artist in the making of just what I've made above. If nothing else, our long nights of dreaming are proof of that. More than six billion minds, from infant to elder, are eager—as darkness floods our planet, zone to zone—to weave the scraps of daily life and inescapable dread and craving into things we later discard or trouble our waking selves to comprehend, sometimes for years: stories that almost answer our hopes of the ultimate reward we've richly earned or that plunge us forever in the fires we've won for a lifetime's meanness or launch us on into mere oblivion, an endless ending.

FURTHER READING

The resources for a study of the life and work of Jesus are literally inexhaustible. No other human being has been more written about; and the poles of that literature might, quite accurately, be described as (at one end) humane and often magisterial scholarship and (at the other) mad and hateful ranting. Both poles are available, in thickets, in any sizable library or bookstore; and as I've indicated above, anyone who writes about Jesus for a substantial number of readers is likely to hear from the ranters more often than the humane masters. The books I suggest below, serious as they are, are sane beginnings but only beginnings. Many great lives have labored to master small corners of this knowledge.

Contemporary efforts to write scrupulously about what has been called, for at least a century, "the historical Jesus"—as distinct from the Jesus of faith—have resulted in a few works of special interest. One of general appeal, written by an eminent scholar of the relations of Jesus to first-century Judaism, is *The His-*

torical Figure of Jesus by E. P. Sanders. Sanders's earlier *Jesus and Judaism* is more daring in its claims and is mostly clear in its complex arguments.

Another, briefer, volume that announces itself as a life is *Jesus: A Revolutionary Biography* by John Dominic Crossan, the most conspicuous member of the Jesus Seminar and one who has remained unfortunately given to—or has permitted his publisher to give—sensation-seeking claims for his work. Yet he's unquestionably a deeply read student of his subject, and portions of his prolific work remain deserving of watchful attention. His brief life of Jesus is short on meat and long on gristle, deriving as it does from his longer *The Historical Jesus: The Life of a Mediterranean Jewish Peasant*; but he sometimes ventilates old assumptions in a provocative way, and his small-boy delight in baiting orthodox Jesus scholars is occasionally amusing.

The most encyclopedic recent effort in the field is appearing under the title *A Marginal Jew*. The author, John P. Meier, has so far published three of a potential four volumes; his learning is immense and his presentation of it is a model of clarity, though his principles of organization are not always apparent. Any serious student of the subject cannot look to Meier for anything resembling a narrative history, but he can hardly ignore the breadth and solidity of Meier's work. If one reads him for nothing else, his exhaustive notes are a guide to hundreds of other sources on virtually every imaginable aspect of Jesus' life and teaching.

Older lives of Jesus by two of the most distinguished British New Testament scholars of the twentieth century are still helpful in the modesty of the claims they make and the resonant wisdom which accompanies their narratives—C. H. Dodd's *The Founder of Christianity* and Vincent Taylor's *The Life and Ministry of Jesus.*

For general information on the four Gospels and the remainder of the earliest Jesus literature, I most often consult three introductions to the New Testament. The more compact and readily usable is *Anatomy of the New Testament* by Robert Spivey and D. Moody Smith. Not only do they proceed to examine each of the documents of the New Testament with unusual sanity and insight, they likewise offer full bibliographies for further reading. And their long chapter on "Jesus the Messiah" is rich and inviting of further thought.

The largest introduction is Raymond Brown's *An Introduction to the New Testament,* the final major work of a distinguished career. More obviously opinionated than Spivey and Moody Smith, Raymond Brown was nonetheless unsurpassed in his knowledge of the territory.

Bart D. Ehrman's *The New Testament: A Historical Introduction to the Early Christian Writings* is a fresh introduction from a younger scholar. While Ehrman pays slim attention to literary and historical concerns, to the crucially important persistence of oral tradition in the early Jesus sect—or to written evidence from the mid–first century—his avoidance of undue solemnity and of needless kowtowing to his seniors are productive of numerous keen perceptions.

Anyone interested in reading further in discussions of the ethics of Jesus could begin with the work of three contemporaries. Stanley Hauerwas is the most eminent, and most controversial, of living Christian ethicists. He is also extraordinarily prolific. *The Hauerwas Reader* is a good introduction to his often surprising, occasionally startling, but frequently inarguable thought.

Richard B. Hays's *The Moral Vision of the New Testament* provides a thorough and fearless reading of the evolution of Jesus' teaching in the hands of his often hapless followers and of what that teaching might mean for serious lives, here and now.

In *What Did Jesus Mean?* Anna Wierzbicka, a linguistic philosopher, goes to extended and often original lengths to analyze the semantics—and therefore the moral, ethical and theological intentions—of Jesus in the Sermon on the Mount and the parables.

The translation of the Bible which I consult most often, for reliability and eloquence, remains the Revised Standard Version (RSV). Unfortunately, it's increasingly difficult to find and has been almost entirely replaced by the considerably less reliable New Revised Standard Version (NRSV). That revision of the RSV, though it claims in its preface to seek "to preserve all that is best in the English Bible as it has been known and used through the years," has—in many places—weakened the prior translation with failures to represent the original languages. The Updated New American Standard Translation (NAS) remains, as I noted above, the most nearly literal version which is also readable—and available—with any degree of ease. The New International Version (NIV) is generally clear, widely available and a good deal less interested in explaining what it takes to be the intent of its Hebrew and Greek originals than other such contemporary versions as the Amplified Bible (AB) and the Revised English Bible (REB).

The latter two, while widely circulated and sometimes of interest, are so involved in attempting to wring interpretations and explanations from the original languages that their guesswork often becomes not a translation but a phantasmagoric paraphrase. I couldn't commend any other widely available modern version, least of all the Good News Bible, another sad paraphrase. The King James Version of 1611, though still much-loved, and obsessively consulted by many conservative and Fundamentalist Christians, is based upon seriously defective original texts; and its seventeenth-century prose, while surpassingly eloquent in many places, is frequently so antiquated as to be beyond comprehension by most modern readers.

APPENDICES

The following poems are referred to in the footnotes on pages 28 and 78.

VISION

I'm sleeping with Jesus and his twelve disciples
On the vacant east shore of Lake Kinnereth—
The Sea of Galilee—near where he exorcised
The demon Legion. We're flat on the ground,
Cocooned in clothes. Mine are light street clothes
(Apparently modern, theirs are classic robes);
And I wake early, well before dawn—
Hour of the worm that desolates hope.
I give it long minutes to line another tunnel
With eggs that will yield the next white wave
Of ravenous heirs.
                            Then I roll to my right side
And see in the frail dark that Jesus has somehow

Moved nearer toward me. I listen to hear
If he sleeps or wakes.
                        Then we stand in the lake,
Both bare to the waist. Light creeps out toward us
From the hills behind; the water's warm.
I see us both as if from a height.
My spine is scored by a twelve-inch incision,
Bracketed now by gentian-purple
Ink that's the map for X-ray therapy
Due in two days. Jesus's beard
Is short and dry, though with both broad hands
He lifts clear water and pours it down
My neck and scar.
                        Then we climb toward shore.
I get there first and wait on the stones—
We're still the only two awake.
Behind me he says "Your sins are forgiven."
I think "That's good but not why I came."
I turn and say "Am I also cured?"
He comes close but looks down. He says "That too,"
Then wades strong past me and touches land.

INSTRUCTION

Throwing the coins down in the Temple Judas
left and going off hanged himself.
                                        Matthew 27.5

I'm given the time it takes to tell you
Precisely this. Ask no questions.
There was one sighting which
Has not been reported by loyalists.
Peter, John, Mary, James
Have milked tears enough with their
Reunions to farm a fair-sized
Salt-lick in Sodom. I don't grudge them
That. The one not reported however
Was to me.
                    I'd got out of town by Friday
Dawn to miss the dustup I launched
In the garden. The cash was slung in my left
Groin, nudging other privates,
For the seven-mile walk to Emmaus—
The inn. We'd never worked that.
I could sleep the hours it would take to kosher
Him white as veal, the loyalists to note they'd
Failed him equally and scuttle home—
Dried boats, nets, wives,
Mothers-in-law. Then I'd head back
To town for the sinecure they'd thrown in
To sweeten the cash—bookkeeper
At the licensed Temple lamb-and-dove
Purveyance: no one cracked a smile.

I'd start Monday morning, under light
Guard till Friday (they had a week's
Worth of anxiety for me; I'd
Known the eleven through a year on the road
And knew I was safe—they'd growl but
On fast feet: Parthian growls).

                             I slept
Two days, waking only to think I'd
Never slept better and gnaw
A flat cake I'd hooked on the way
And ask if the rest—alluvial mud—
Wasn't better reward than cash or job
Or memory of Peter's white face
In fireshine, slick with fright:
Blown hog's bladder burst
By boys (the answer was Yes and I'd sleep
Again).

                  Sunday evening I was sated but
Hungry. I skimmed my eyes with cool
Dry fingers, rehung the privates
And went down to eat in the common room—
Loud clutch of Passover pilgrims
Bound north, no face I knew.
I'd finished when another three entered
And sat—Klopas, his squat wife, a trim
Tan stranger. The Klopases had bankrolled
Us, steady but stingy, through Galilee.
My legs jerked to leave, then locked me
In. I was legal; I'd make my first
Stand here. But they talked to the stranger
And never looked up. I licked at
My bowl and filled my space—paid-up patron.

The window over them faced due-
West, so I fixed on that and bathed
In sunset.
           The girl brought their food.
They groveled to bless it. The stranger stood,
Neat as a sprout sucked up in a morning.
It was him, no question—crammed-
Down, a little ashy at the gills but
Pleasant and coming toward me.
I tried again to rise in the days
It took him to reach my bench;
Legs refused.
           His hands were ruined—
Brown holes, barely dry—
But otherwise fit. I begged not to touch
Them, though I didn't speak.
He kept silent too,
His hands at his thighs.
No pause or stare, the smile
Never quit. He bent
To my hair and pressed it once, quite lengthily,
With a mouth that seemed his usual mouth—
No stars or rays, no sizzling brand—
Then walked the breadth of the floor and out.
I had not had to touch him—
Not direct, not skin.
I waited for roars, leaps, laughs
From the room. Klopas and his wife were chewing
In tears, drowned in the gift.
No one else had looked.
I sat till the next gnat
Sapped my heel, then stood as I was—

Freed to stand into honor like rain—
And went through the same door,
Same empty yard.
      Halfway back
To town in dark dry as meal, I
Groped out a tree that promised to hold.
Honor had lasted a full three miles.
I lasted a full two minutes
By the neck, longer than planned—my well-oiled belt
(The privates were insufficient ballast).
Nobody claimed body or ballast;
We two were the bachelors.
        You may now ask questions.

REYNOLDS PRICE

Reynolds Price was born in Macon, North Carolina in 1933. Educated at Duke University and, as a Rhodes Scholar, at Merton College, Oxford University, he has taught at Duke since 1958 and is now James B. Duke Professor of English.

His first short stories, and many later ones, are published in his *Collected Stories*. *A Long and Happy Life* was published in 1962 and won the William Faulkner Award for a best first novel. *Kate Vaiden* was published in 1986 and won the National Book Critics Circle Award. *The Good Priest's Son* in 2005 was his fourteenth novel. Among his thirty-seven volumes are further collections of fiction, poetry, plays, essays and translations. Price is a member of both the American Academy of Arts and Letters and the American Academy of Arts and Sciences, and his work has been translated into seventeen languages.